Interpreting Life

The House of Prisca and Aquila

Our mission at the House of Prisca and Aquila is to produce quality books that expound accurately the word of God to empower women and men to minister together in a multicultural church. Our writers have a positive view of the Bible as God's revelation that affects both thoughts and words, so it is plenary, historically accurate, and consistent in itself; fully reliable; and authoritative as God's revelation. Because God is true, God's revelation is true, inclusive to men and women and speaking to a multicultural church, wherein all the diversity of the church is represented within the parameters of egalitarianism and inerrancy.

The word of God is what we are expounding, thereby empowering women and men to minister together in all levels of the church and home. The reason we say women and men together is because that is the model of Prisca and Aquila, ministering together to another member of the church—Apollos: "Having heard Apollos, Priscilla and Aquila took him aside and more accurately expounded to him the Way of God" (Acts 18:26). True exposition, like true religion, is by no means boring—it is fascinating. Books that reveal and expound God's true nature "burn within us" as they elucidate the Scripture and apply it to our lives.

This was the experience of the disciples who heard Jesus on the road to Emmaus: "Were not our hearts burning while Jesus was talking to us on the road, while he was opening the scriptures to us?" (Luke 24:32). We are hoping to create the classics of tomorrow: significant and accessible trade and academic books that "burn within us."

Our "house" is like the home to which Prisca and Aquila no doubt brought Apollos as they took him aside. It is like the home in Emmaus where Jesus stopped to break bread and reveal his presence. It is like the house built on the rock of obedience to Jesus (Matt 7:24). Our "house," as a euphemism for our publishing team, is a home where truth is shared and Jesus' Spirit breaks bread with us, nourishing all of us with his bounty of truth.

We are delighted to work together with Wipf and Stock in this series and welcome submissions on a wide variety of topics from an egalitarian inerrantist global perspective. The House of Prisca and Aquila is also a ministry center affiliated with the International Council of Community Churches.

For more information, visit www.houseofpriscaandaquila.com.

Interpreting Life

Christian Women's Roles in the Church and Home

PATRICIA C. BURKE

WIPF & STOCK · Eugene, Oregon

INTERPRETING LIFE
Christian Women's Roles in the Church and Home

Wipf & Stock
An Imprint of Wipf and Stock Publishers
199 W. 8th Ave., Suite 3
Eugene, OR 97401
www.wipfandstock.com

ISBN 13: 978-1-60899-528-8

Manufactured in the U.S.A.

Contents

Preface

It's quite clear. If I am no good to him, if I am merely a doll, a wife, and not a human being—then it is all useless and I don't want to carry on this existence. Of course, I am idle, but I am not idle by nature; I simply haven't yet discovered what I can do here. . . . I know he is brilliant, poetic, and intelligent, full of power, but it annoys me that he should look at everything from a gloomy angle. I sometimes want to break loose from his somewhat sombre influence, to ignore it—but I can't. His influence is to see things with his eyes, and I am afraid of losing my own self and yet not becoming like him.

—SOPHIE TOLSTOY[1]

THESE WORDS OF SOPHIE Tolstoy signify how perplexing life is for a woman who tries to find meaning solely through her husband and children. Sophie evidently had a stormy marriage and spent most of her life trying to understand her talented husband, as so many of us women do. She respected him for his brilliance and power, yet tired of his darker side. On the one hand, she wanted to be like him; on the other, there were times when she wanted to leave him and save herself. Her experience fits the modern cliché regarding men that I hear so often from women: We can't live with them and we can't live without them. From 1862 to 1865, when Sophie was eighteen to twenty-one, before she became absorbed with her thirteen children, she had time to write, and the topic that consumed her was her relationship with her husband.

> I am a source of satisfaction to him, a nurse, a piece of furniture, a woman—nothing more. I try to suppress all human feelings in myself. The thing to do is not to love, to be clever and sly, and to hide all one's bad points. . . . [S]ee what I have done by loving him so deeply. It is so painful and humiliating, but he thinks that it is merely silly.[2]

1. S. Tolstoy, in Moffatt and Painter, *Revelations*, 139.
2. Ibid., 144.

Like so many women born before and after Sophie wrote these words, she developed a persona that was acceptable to her husband but, in the process, lost her own self. During her childrearing years, Sophie described herself as quite happy, but then in 1890, when she was forty-six years old and her focus on her children had lessened, her gloomy side returned:

> I am so used to living not my own life, but the life of Lyova and the children, that I feel I have wasted my day if I haven't done something for them. It is sad that my emotional dependence on the man I love should have killed so much of my energy and ability; there was certainly once a great deal of energy in me.[3]

Had Sophie lived today, she would likely have been diagnosed by a prominent psychotherapist as having some form of depression and treated with Prozac or Zoloft, and possibly would never have written the words that have helped some modern women understand the risks involved when one is totally dependent, both financially and emotionally, on a man for support.

In the twentieth century, we had the writings of Anne Morrow Lindbergh to illustrate the confusion and frustration felt within women who were living their lives nearly exclusively for their husbands and children. In her well-known book, *Gift from the Sea*, Lindbergh writes about her discovery that she was not alone in grappling with how to live a meaningful, fulfilling life within the traditional role assigned women in our society:

> Even those whose lives had appeared to be ticking imperturbably under their smiling clock-faces were often trying, like me, to evolve another rhythm with more creative pauses in it, more adjustment to their individual needs, and new and more alive relationships to themselves as well as others.[4]

Anne Lindbergh was privileged enough to escape occasionally to the beach and dwell on her own life. Because of her affluence, her writings were published and preserved. How many other women, though, were there in the past and are here today, begging to be heard, but who have no opportunity? Very few diaries of women were made public before the twentieth century, so it is impossible to know how many frustrated

3. Ibid., 147.
4. Lindbergh, *Gift from the Sea*, 8.

women have been crying out for understanding since the beginning of recorded history. I would never have discovered these women if I had not had similar feelings and chosen to use writing, as did the women above, as a means of making sense of the uncertainties in my own life.

Along the path I followed, I discovered the stories of many women who had great potential and dreams of doing something worthwhile with their lives, other than caring for their husbands and children, but who were not able to follow those dreams because women had yet to be recognized as having anything other than nurturing abilities to offer to the world. In most instances, the women's writings were buried for years because they were not given a medium through which to tell their stories. With this book, I am hoping to make amends to our forgotten female legacy and share their words, along with mine and other women's thoughts I have encountered along the way, so that the next generation of "submissive" women might find the path to a worthwhile life somewhat easier to tread.

WRITING THERAPY

Over the past thirty-four years, I have kept a journal to help me make sense out of life's problems and contradictions. When a problem becomes too difficult to solve and I have no one with whom to discuss it, I turn to writing. Unless I take the time to record my private thoughts, I continue to dwell on the subject, getting more and more agitated and frustrated. But once I put the thoughts on paper, my life makes sense, for a short time at least. In this manner, I have tracked my thought process through many life stages and crises and have avoided making numerous relationship and career mistakes. In the 1980s, when word processors became popular, I began to call my diary entries "memos to myself."

What is significant about the memos I write? Some people go to therapists and pour out their stories to a sympathetic ear or join support groups and share with those who have similar experiences. Others use friends and ministers as sounding boards. Writing is my therapy, taking me in a few minutes from feeling overwhelmed and disgusted with life to being on top of the world because once again my place on the planet makes sense. Through the writing of memos, engaging in academic research and writing, reading biographies, and interviewing contemporary women, most of my questions regarding my own life mysteries have been answered. From the voices of other women, my thoughts took shape, but, in the process, many more questions regarding the nature of women in general arose, and I delved deeper to understand more completely the unfolding of women's development from childhood to old age. I discovered that psychological interpretations are extremely limiting and that to truly understand women's progression through life stages requires a broader look at social and historical issues over a longer time period. My task grew to unmanageable proportions, so, to ensure the completion of my doctoral work, I narrowed my search to the study of identity development in professional women, looking closely at the intersection of work and family in married women. I was especially interested in the role of work in women's definitions of themselves. Do women describe themselves primarily by who they are as wives, mothers, daughters, and sisters, the roles they have traditionally played in society, or do they also define themselves, as men do, through what they accomplish—their work?

Over a six-year period, beginning in the early 1990s, I interviewed more than sixty women in New England and in London. Forty-five of these women's stories were included in a dissertation on women's identity that was completed in 1994. Since that time, I have continued to interview women as I encounter those who have an interesting story to tell. These women's ages range from thirty-two to ninety-nine, so most of the adult lifespan is represented; their work lives vary from picking cotton in the 1930s to practicing criminal law and medicine in the twentieth and twenty-first centuries. Caucasian women from America and England, as well as African-American, Jamaican, and Latino women, have openly shared their captivating stories with me.

Because I use a storytelling methodology designed to arrive at concepts regarding women's identity, I have been rewarded with what researchers refer to as rich descriptions of the women's lives. Concepts never before encountered have surfaced, leaving me with new insights into how women interpret or make sense of their lives. In addition to the interviews, I disciplined myself to use my discretionary reading time on women's biographies, autobiographies, and historical accounts of women's journeys through time. Also, in the classes I was teaching at the university level, I continually came upon new perspectives through my students from different cultures.

One of the unanswered questions regarding my research findings was: How applicable are my findings to other women like myself, that is, evangelical Christian women? Throughout the interviewing of these sixty-plus women, I had many "aha" experiences where I said to myself (usually in a memo) that a particular woman had the same thoughts or feelings as I did regarding my role in society or my place in the home. In spite of the fact that these women appeared to have nothing in common with me, their life stories helped me answer some of the questions I was asking myself about women's roles. So, what exactly was going on here? Why was I seeing these patterns? I thought my personal problems stemmed from my childhood upbringing and the conservative Christian church to which I belonged. But these women were from many different religious heritages and we were telling the same story.

So, I looked more closely at the women's backgrounds. I primarily interviewed educated, professional women who were engaged in a dual career-and-family lifestyle. These women were articulate and eager to share their stories because they were members of the first cohort in our society to have access to careers that had always been dominated by men. They had fought for and acquired a place in the world where they felt useful and admired for their contributions to society outside the home, and yet they were also wives and mothers. The majority of the women had a childhood religious affiliation or indoctrination. In other words, they were brought up by parents who embraced and taught their children a particular set of religious beliefs. Many of the women had also attended parochial schools as a child and adolescent.

Among the women I interviewed, around two-thirds considered themselves to be a member of a religious organization (both Christian and Jewish), but not necessarily the same religious affiliation as their parents. Some were not active participants in a religious institution, but were engaged in a spiritual search that stemmed from the contradictions they felt between their childhood belief system and the one they had acquired as adults. Being affiliated with a religious institution did not mean the women were active participants. This was especially true of some of the Catholic women who described themselves as being Irish Catholic, Polish Catholic, or Italian Catholic. Being Catholic was perceived as a component of one's ethnicity. Only one woman interviewed had a formal association with a Jewish organization and she called herself a "spiritual Jew."

The religious experiences of the women I studied were so varied that nothing was initially noteworthy, but there were some interesting commonalities regarding these women's childhood socialization that could help explain their religious choices in adulthood. Those who were born after World War II, came of age during the chaotic times of the 1960s and 1970s, and had attended college during those years were all quite similar to each other. They had read some of the same books, heard some of the same speakers on their campuses, and generally experienced the craziness of demonstrations and riots. But perhaps the most noteworthy, these wild times offered much contrast to their rather mild, happy childhoods in the 1950s.

Therefore, one of the most fascinating discoveries for me was the importance of looking at a person's cohort to understand their personal development. Cohort is derived from the date of birth and the time in history when the women came of age. For the women mentioned above, being in adolescence and young adulthood during the chaotic social movements in the 1960s and 1970s offered the necessary contrast and contradiction, and often crises, to set in motion conditions that resulted in much introspection and, consequently, significant personal growth.

Cohort was obviously influential in my own development process. I went in 1963 from a peaceful, free life on the farm into a world that was being turned upside down by the social upheaval of the time. My strong, conservative Christian values stood in stark contrast to what I was experiencing as I reached late adolescence and young adulthood, the stage when individuals make the decision to confirm or cast away what their parents have taught them. Through the study of cohort differences, I discovered the link between my own life process and Christian women in general, realizing that each new cohort needs to recognize the impact that culture has on their development, which, in turn, influences decisions they make about key relationships, work, and family.

Bonnie F. Miller-McLemore adds insight about the effect of cohort on women's development. Each time a cohort of women in the past two hundred years has attempted to address women's social issues, that specific movement targeted a very narrow segment of women in society. For example, in the twentieth century, there was a cohort of women who were "submerged in the lore of idealized motherhood and femininity that captured the American imagination in the 1950s with unheralded vigor."[5] Few of the women who came of age during the 1950s were even aware of the earlier work in women's rights. Because the times mandated it, they were busy attempting to be perfect wives and mothers, or, if working-class

5. Miller-McLemore, *Also a Mother*, 69.

or poor women, simply trying to survive life's daily grind. The twentieth-century movement targeted the white, educated professional women in society and "lost touch with the critical stream of thought and experiences of working-class mothers and mothers of color."[6] The emphasis during that movement was on political and legal rights of women, and the initial setting was the workplace. Feminists soon learned that women could not gain equality in the workplace without having it first at home. An equal relationship between men and women in the home is the foundation for women achieving freedom in other areas of life.

In the twenty-first century, this egalitarian relationship in marriages is becoming more evident among educated, professional families, possibly because responsibilities outside the home and salaries are more equal, but a large segment of our society has gained little, if anything, from the equality movement because their marriage and family lives still adhered to constricting values and norms. And I believe that many of these women who did not benefit from the women's movement were Christian women. They were operating from what they understood to be the Biblical edict to be submissive, and, consequently, their personal needs were suppressed. We were led to believe that feminists were a negative influence in our society and to be avoided at all cost, not realizing the complexity of what was happening to women's and men's roles. Consequently, many of us did not change at all, and those who did experienced much confusion and pain brought about from being among the first women to challenge the narrow interpretation of women's roles in the home and church.

Twenty years later, after completing my research on women and arriving at a rather unstructured but meaningful framework for understanding the development process of women, I began to use my findings to help other women who were struggling with their identities. The women most difficult to help were the Christian women because of their early indoctrination on the role of women in the church and home. Christian women were socialized to sacrifice themselves to care for others; any other behavior was suspect. Being selfish or self-centered are some adjectives that come to mind. Regardless of what we were thinking or writing in our private worlds, we never let on that we had unfulfilled needs of our own. We were trained to be nurturers, and we would die happy if we could make it through life without destroying that image.

6. Ibid., 67.

For many of us, and for many reasons, that image was shattered and much damage was done to Christian women, men, and their families when years of repressed conflict bubbled to the surface in the form of intense marital conflicts, divorce, and abusive relationships. As I personally encountered more and more of these altered lives, I became determined to share what I had learned in the past four decades from my own struggles. From the pain and suffering we encounter in daily living, we are forced to question who we are and where we are headed, and, from that questioning, we finally act, discard outgrown ways of handling our world, and create a new life. Ordinarily, when Christians speak of creating a new life, they are referring to their initial conversion experience, but that experience alone is not supposed to be the end of the process. Instead, it is the beginning of a new life. Christ gives us a push in the right direction, but expects us to cooperate with the Holy Spirit to become the mature person who is acceptable to Christ.

AUTOBIOGRAPHICAL APPROACH

Because my search process began in 1976 as a deep personal need to understand the role of Christian women in society, I decided to begin this book where I started, using questions raised in my writings and my own developmental pathway as a springboard for helping other women interpret their lives. My journey from adolescence to midlife was extremely complicated because I was trying to merge two separate worlds, which were exceedingly contradictory to each other. On one hand, I was brought up in a home and a wider culture that adhered to the belief that woman's place is in the home. To reinforce that view, when I was nineteen, I married a man from the same religious background, who was, for the first half of our marriage, a minister, placing our family in a glass-house setting. We had no choice but to adhere to the narrow confines of the church and family where women were primarily a support system for men and children. On the other hand, I was a child, and later an adult, with a dream to do something extraordinary with my life: a vision that could not be fulfilled if I were tied to the stringent role of being a fulltime wife and mother. The inability to fulfill that dream triggered many years of confusion and frustration with the nurturing role I had assumed and, in addition, created many problems in my marriage.

One of the first truths I discovered from my own journey and from my involvement with other individuals is that seldom, if ever, does an individual go through life following a preconceived plan of action that does not require continual modification of one's childhood dream. I now know that what I heard many times in my early life and finally admitted in my mid-thirties is true: Life is unpredictable and extraordinarily hard for nearly everyone. But what I never fully understood was that the hardships are precisely what make life interesting and fulfilling. Without these bumps in the road, we would remain forever as children. From these hurdles, in the form of interpersonal conflicts, failed or shaky relationships, lost jobs, illnesses, deaths, financial problems, and on and on, we learn who we truly are and what our role in life is.

The things that happen along the way play a significant role as well. If nothing else, they offer contrast to the blows we receive and help us gradually define what we find most important in life. And, in this manner, though I am oversimplifying the interpretation, each of us becomes a mature adult and an authentic person, that is, a person who lives from his or her self-selected values rather than those prescribed by others, whether in the church or society in general.

PURPOSE OF THE BOOK

In an effort to help other women understand their own life process, I expose my own ignorance, naiveté, idealism, and near disastrous mistakes. The questions I was asking were not new, but I thought they were. They were questions that have been asked since the beginning of time: Where did I come from, who am I, and what do I want to do with my life? These questions are not gender-specific. Both men and women have voiced them quietly to themselves and to others throughout the history of humankind. But, more recent historians have discovered that women have been asking themselves an additional set of questions: How can I do what I want to do with my life and still fulfill the expectations others have of me? Can I be a good wife and mother and a unique, independent woman? Can I nurture and support the goals of my husband and children, take care of my parents and in-laws as they age, be a proud and responsive grandparent, and yet satisfy my inner needs that are separate from those of the other people in my life? Generally, what I was asking was: What is a woman's role in the world? More specifically, what is a Christian woman's place in society, the home, and the church?

Sprinkled throughout the book are tidbits of information that I gleaned from women I encountered during my quest—some with struggles similar to mine and others whose challenges were quite different, including stories from our female legacy from the eighteenth century on, and from contemporary women whose struggles and questioning of their role in society, along with their joys and successes, helped me answer questions related to being a woman in our particular place in history. Without the stories of other women, I would never have pieced together an interpretation of my own life. I now have, in addition to a translation of my own life, a deeper understanding of what it means to be female in the past and in the present. And, through the long process of understanding myself, I have found my niche—an ability to help other women navigate life. Hopefully, this book will contribute to that purpose.

It must be stressed here that this is one interpretation only. It is an explanation, at the time of the writing, of what I think happened in my life and in the lives of others I have encountered. It is important to make some kind of sense out of our lives. There is a beginning, a middle, and an ending, at least a temporary one, composed of life events that now make sense because of knowledge gained along the path called life.

I believe that what I have to say is important because I speak as a Christian woman who has chosen to remain in the church in spite of a series of life events that some would consider destructive to the individual and the marriage. I struggled with my faith because of many contradictions that I observed in the teachings and practice of my church. I was considered less than a Christian because I was different from the other, more traditional women. For example, I did not enjoy teaching children, preparing food for church dinners, sitting in business meetings, and sitting in Bible classes that had nothing to do with my practical life and the issues with which I was struggling. I was considered a feminist because I suggested that women might rather do something different for the church than what they normally did at home, such as program planning and teaching of adults, instead of cleaning the church building and preparing food. For more than forty years, as an adult, I have sat quietly in the pew listening to men, both intelligent and not-so-intelligent ones, present their opinions of the Scriptures while many intelligent women kept silent. The initial reason I remained in the church was to save my marriage and not to confuse my children. But, in the process, I became my own unique person, and determined for myself what I believe God is saying to me and how he wants me to serve.

1

Questioning Life

IN 1976, I BEGAN to wonder when it would be my turn to do something meaningful with my life, to explore the world outside my small realm of work, family, and church. At that point, I began to contemplate what I wanted to do when my husband, Gary, finished his graduate work and could support the family without my assistance—that was what we thought would happen. I was thirty-two years old, had a couple of college degrees, and yet had been in a support mode for the past thirteen years. My husband's education and career goals were our sole consideration, and my job was to make sure he accomplished his goals. To do so, I worked full-time outside the home in an eight-to-five job and spent the evenings and weekends trying to make order out of the chaos that resulted from a busy family of five. When I began writing in 1976, our three children were ages seven, three, and eight months. I was exhausted, unfulfilled, and disillusioned with life.

Somehow during my upbringing, I had decided I was special. No one told me that; I just knew I was meant to do something out of the ordinary with my life, in spite of the fact that there was little encouragement for a girl born during World War II, living on an isolated farm in Colorado, to do anything other than marry and have children. I had formed a foggy notion that I would do something quite different with my life. I had few thoughts of getting married. By the time I reached high school, I had a dream of going to India, working independently, buying myself a piano, and then, by about age twenty-six, I would marry a charming person who did not interfere with my fulfilling life. I remained emphatic about my plans through high school graduation. Most of the girls in my class cried at the graduation ceremony because they thought their life had ended. I felt mine was just beginning and looked forward to getting out of that small town and seeing the world.

A few months later, I left for college—a Christian environment—and entered a world that slightly resembled a dark, foggy night in a black-and-white movie. I was scared, timid, and compliant; I caved in to what others suggested I do, which included getting engaged to a young man who planned to be a minister. At one time, I tried to break off the relationship, knowing I was not ready for such a commitment, but the Christian college cultural expectation for every woman there was to find a man to marry. That was why most of the young women were there. I was too weak to resist because my own identity and life goals had not yet been formulated. My dream of becoming an independent, out-of-the ordinary woman faded into the background and remained buried until I entered my thirties. Since I had no identity of my own, I was faithfully doing what my husband and others expected of a young Christian wife. The question I later had to answer was: *What happened to that strong, focused young woman? How could I get so far off track from my original plans?*

SETTING THE STAGE

For the first thirty years of my life, I floated along basically *unaware of myself as a unique person* with needs of my own that had to be met. My first two years were spent on my grandparents' cotton farm in Texas, waiting for my dad to return from World War II. There, I was taken care of by an older brother (twenty months older), an aunt or two, my mother, and grandparents. I can recall no memories from this period of my life. This is not unusual, of course, because I was only seventeen months old when my dad returned from the war and my family moved to Colorado where my dad and some of his cousins were getting a new start in life. I remember one story my mother told about how well I could talk at the time, because I said to my grandmother just as we were leaving to go to Colorado, "Mammy, get your bonnet." And that was all I was ever told about my first two years of life.

During the next sixteen years, I lived on several farms where my dad and mother worked from dawn to dusk to make a decent life for their family. Nearly everyone I knew from those years were farm people, and, though I did not know it then, farm families are in a social class of their own. We lived in a world of our own making, and what was happening in the larger world was of little concern to us. Farmers by nature are self-sufficient and independent people who learn to survive without help from anyone except each other and their banker. The only time we received any financial assistance was when my dad went to the bank each spring to borrow money to buy seeds and fertilizer for the next year's crop. Then, in the fall, when the crops were harvested, he paid off the bank and we survived until another spring.

Although life was exceptionally hard for farmers and their wives, I felt practically none of the stress and knew little of the hardships my parents experienced. I do remember how devastating rains were when they came at the wrong time of the year, and how, occasionally, my dad would lose all his crops because of hail. During those times, I believe the government helped out with what we call today "disaster relief" funds. I was never aware of being poor because my parents did not believe it was smart to discuss money problems around your children. My mother reminded me of that often when I had children of my own. Also, we had no television or glossy magazines to build materialistic expectations. I remember getting very few Christmas presents. My usual present was a store-purchased skirt and sweater, which were special to me because my mother made most of my clothes. When I was a young child, my clothes were made out of feed sacks, the bags that flour came in. Later, my mother would purchase fabric and sew late at night when everyone else was relaxing. I guess we were deprived, but I never felt different from my friends; they were also farmers' sons and daughters.

Practically nothing from early childhood stands out. My life as a school-age child and teenager revolved mainly around my friends in school. I was a good student, rather popular, and always busy during the school year with homework and reading. I remember my mother telling me how I was lucky (not smart) because I made good grades with little effort. I bought her argument for many years. Girls were not supposed to be intelligent.

During the summer, I worked for my mother with no mention of being paid for the work, and read and played the piano when I could steal some time away from the housework. The novels I devoured, many of them stories of Christian young women, showed me another, more exciting world, one I planned to enter when I was grown.

OUT OF THE NEST—INTO THE WORLD

My life changed drastically when I graduated from high school in 1962 and followed my brother to a small Christian college in the South. My parents had always gone to church two or three times a week for as long as I could remember, and someone must have convinced my parents that we should attend a Christian college. I received a small academic scholarship and left home, totally unprepared for the world I was about to enter.

The atmosphere in the Christian college was very "churchy" compared to the way I grew up. The church we attended in my hometown was an extension of our family. We studied the Bible and sang church songs, but the only ministers I heard were those who came from the South to hold gospel meetings once a year. My parents socialized primarily with people from the church, leaving me with no contrasting experience to arrive at a true understanding of what *The Church* was. I believe I experienced culture shock during the year I was away from home attending the Christian college. Twice on Sundays and once on Wednesday evenings, we attended extremely large, well-furnished churches. The people dressed much more nicely than I had ever seen before, and the services were rather formal. I think that was the beginning of my feeling different from the people with whom I had spent many decades associating. It was there that I donned my first mask, a persona that made me *appear* to be like others.

At this college, I met the man I would marry at age nineteen. Gary was a senior when I was a freshman. We were introduced by my brother, who had known Gary for two or three years. We started dating immediately upon my arrival at college and, at Christmastime, he gave me an engagement ring. I feel now that I was in a stupor during that year, going to classes, just doing what everyone else was doing, without being conscious that my future was being formed by a culture that I could not even begin to comprehend. I discovered much later that it was not just me who was in a fog. Throughout society, women were making decisions to marry without giving them much thought. Years later, in some of my research notes, I noted the story of Olivia,[1] a stay-at-home mom whose husband made enough money so that she never had to work outside the home:

1. With the exception of my family members and authors, nearly all names in this book are pseudonyms.

Olivia mentions just "going with the flow" all her life, especially since marriage. She has recently realized that she didn't actually choose her husband, even. They dated for six years, she became more a part of his family, modeled after his mother (a housewife), and never questioned it until recently (after twelve or thirteen years of marriage).

I almost think that I really didn't have an opinion. I never realized that you could think about this, you know. I was anesthetized not to think.

I have been writing . . . and not knowing why. I just assumed it was because there is no adult contact now. I just talk to myself.

Olivia is attempting to find herself through her writing. She feels that a geographical move—from a secure, social neighborhood to one where houses are far apart and she has no daily contact with neighbors, or anyone else, other than her children and husband—has pushed her "into talking about deeper things" with her best friend.

Olivia's situation did not surprise me, because we shared some similarities in our life paths, but when I interviewed Wilma, an African American woman from the Bronx, I was completely surprised to find that she had also stumbled into marriage in the 1960s with little thought as to the consequences of her action:

I stayed with my grandparents as I was trying to figure out what I was going to do. Got a job at the telephone company which they thought was safe . . . a good job. . . . I was taking Russian and a chemistry class. Still in a my-heart-belongs-to-somebody-somewhere kind of mode.

And then, I met my first husband, who was going to school. He was an adult, was five and a half years older than I was, working full-time in a drafting position and trying to finish up his undergraduate degree at City College. This was a young man who had come from the South, had gone into the Navy, and was really trying to make something out of his life. I just bought that, hook, line, and sinker. I loved that; I loved people who were motivated, and what could I do to help.

Also, during that era, you know, in terms of black consciousness, what was going on in terms of relationships between black men and black women and . . . the notion of being pulled together to support each other during the tough times, so you got into that self-sacrifice mode, so you say, "I'll put my desires and my wishes behind because my husband should go first," and you know, the African American male should be elevated because he is getting beat up all the time, and if you run into somebody who really is trying to make something of himself, then let's help accelerate that process.

Wilma's story was strikingly comparable to mine. In August 1963, Gary and I got married in a small church in my hometown in Colorado. The wedding itself is a blur because of the chaos associated with the arrangements for the big event. Some of the interactions with my husband immediately following the wedding are burned in my memory, though, because of the peculiarity I associated with them. One was that, on our wedding night, my husband, who had just graduated from college with training to become a minister and wanted to get his marriage started right, decided we should read Ephesians 5:21–31. Although his intentions were good, the timing was not right, because I was so overwhelmed by all that had happened to me in the past few months. In addition to starting college and making wedding plans, I had completed a crash course in speedwriting so I could put my husband through graduate school (his dad's suggestion), and, just prior to my wedding, had spent four days and nights sick with a high fever from a severe case of strep throat. I had gotten out of bed one day and married the next, so it was a marvel that I had not collapsed during the ceremony. Here I was, at last, alone with the man whom I would spend the rest of my life with, and he decided to read Ephesians 5. I may have wondered what I had gotten myself into, but had no idea of the magnitude of the issue of submission and what it might mean to me a few years later when our society began to change.

I also had no conception of what it meant to be a minister's wife. Perhaps if I had not been married so young, I would have continued my education at the Christian college where we met and, along the way, would have been better prepared for what was looming. A life of total self-sacrifice was ahead, and I had no idea how all-encompassing this expectation was. Recently, going through some of my mother's old papers, I discovered an article from *The Christian Worker* along with some of my freshman Bible course notes. It was written In February 1963, the year we were married, and described the expectations for the position I was about to assume:

> One of the most commendable services a woman may render is to be a faithful member of the Lord's church and to serve as a helpmate to a gospel preacher. She must support him in hours of weakness—not forgetting the difficulties he encounters, praying for his success as a minister to God's people and a father and

husband. To be a minister's wife requires an unselfish spirit and a willingness to sacrifice; young women who consider marrying ministers should fully understand this.

A minister's wife must closely associate herself with his work and duties; she must not forget in doing this, that her family must share her time too. As a mother and helpmate for her ministering husband she will have little spare time as many women of her acquaintance.[2]

The nearly exclusive focus on the minister's welfare was not unusual for the times. In the early 1960s, the social movement that eventually brought to light the unfairness of women's inferior status in society had not yet surfaced. In the next paragraph, though, the writer warned the wife what it would be like for her:

She must guard against assuming more than her strength will permit. This is very essential since it happens occasionally that some congregation feels [sic] that when a minister is employed that one salary hires both the minister and his wife.

God bless her, with all these expectations she must never forget that she lives in a "glass house" and that her husband is expected to first serve the congregation and secondly his family. Still, people will expect her to be a friendly, considerate, cheerful person, and nothing is more harmful to a minister's influence than a "snobbish" wife always imposing on those whom her husband serves to the best of his ability. An unruly family is very crippling to a minister's success.

The writer explained that the husband should try to understand the stress put on the wife. And, since he would be gone from home so much, when he was at home, it would be necessary for both of them to work hard to ensure that the "home duties be faithfully discharged." The next paragraph is something I came to understand very well later, but at the time had no idea my life would be under such scrutiny.

A woman should possess an education at least equal to that of the average member to be at ease. She will set an example in manners, dress, and speech in the congregation where he labors. In 1 Timothy 3:11 we find the qualifications of a deacon's wife which is also excellent advice for a minister's wife. "Even so must their wives be grave, not slanderers, sober, faithful in all things."[3]

2. Edmonds, "The Minister's Wife," 3.
3. Ibid., 6.

Grave? Sober? Neither of these adjectives described me. I was a free-spirited, energetic person with a goal to change the world. I thought the man I married had the same goal; that was why I became interested in him. The article ended by quoting portions of three Scriptures on submission: Ephesians 5, Colossians 3:18, and 1 Peter 3:1.

> Ephesians 5 gives the finest advice that any wife may have need to digest, "Wives submit yourselves unto your own husbands as unto the Lord. For the husband is the head of the wife, even as Christ is the head of the church: and he is the savior of the body." The inspired account continues, "Therefore, as the church is subject unto Christ, so let the wives be to their husbands in everything."
>
> Col. 3:18: "Wives submit yourselves unto your own husbands, as it is fit in the Lord."
>
> From 1 Pet. 3:1 we read: "Likewise, ye wives, be in subjection to your own husbands, that, if any obey not in word, they may also without the word be won by the conversation of the wives."[4]

These excerpts revealed only part of the story, of course, using a common technique of taking Scripture out of context to make a point. In Ephesians, what was left out was the advice for all Christians to "be subject to *one another* out of reverence for Christ,"[5] and, for the husband, four verses telling him how to love his wife. When discussing the Colossians passage, the article again left out the statement about husbands. In 1 Peter 3, only a small portion of the paragraph on submission was included. At the time, I probably noticed nothing unusual about this, because I had listened all my life to preachers discuss the wife's need to be in submission without mentioning at all the husband's responsibility.[6]

Would any woman wish to marry a minister if she knew before the decision was made that she was to sacrifice all personal freedom and goals? Yes, I believe even I, at age 18, when making the decision to marry, would have felt this was a worthy life to live, not realizing that all women are not cut from the same cloth and that I was not meant to be a minister's wife. My dream, and Gary's, was to go to a foreign country;

---

4. Ibid.

5. This is the King James Version, which was used in the churches I attended as a child. The phrase "be subject to" is burned on my mind.

6. In the church in which I grew up in, the word *preacher* was always used. The terms *minister* and *pastor* were used for more formal churches.

before our marriage, we had discussed becoming missionaries. I had not made the connection that should have been obvious: To be a missionary, you must be a minister's wife, and to be a minister's wife, you must sacrifice personal goals. Perhaps I thought we would end up in India, a country that held much fascination for me.

For the next fourteen years, Gary and I focused on acquiring an education that would prepare us to live a selfless life ministering to others' needs. Gary had planned this before we met, and without any discussion regarding my own needs, his life plan became mine. After both of us received master's degrees and I thought we would settle down, Gary decided to pursue a doctorate in religion, and I, without hesitation, agreed to work while he completed it. It was supposed to take four years; instead, it took eleven. But, our life continued in a fairly normal fashion for a young student family. Gary worked part-time and went to school; I worked full-time and kept the family running smoothly. A daughter was born before Gary went back to school, and two sons came along three years apart when Gary was in the middle of his degree program.

I think now that my early years on the farm helped me develop into a strong, resilient person. Even though I felt at times like a robot—I simply pushed a button and kept moving—I assumed that was the way I was supposed to live. My parents had always worked hard, and so should I. That was my legacy; I was a farmer's daughter, as a later diary entry indicated:

> As I get older, I find myself thinking more and more about my roots, and I frequently define myself as a farmer's daughter. I'm not sure when I started labeling myself in this way, but I think I know why I do it. . . .
>
> I'm a farmer's daughter because I was so fond of my dad, and I lost him at the hand of a drunken driver when I was only twenty-three. I was just getting to know him as an adult, but after his death, my vision of him became even more enhanced—I could see no wrong in him. He was then, and I guess will always be, my hero. . . . He was a farmer; I was proud to be called his daughter; therefore, being a farmer's daughter is a good thing in my mind. The term also implies freedom. I was, on the farm, allowed to be a free spirit. I had some work to do, but I was free to do it as I wanted and when I wanted (within a certain time frame—before my mother came home from the fields). The adult me, therefore, is a hard worker, but one who likes to work very hard for a short time period and then do as I please the rest of the day. Somehow, that approach does not always work in the real world.

In 1976, eight or nine months after my last child was born, I suddenly began to question the life I had been leading. With this came the urge to write, to record my feelings regarding what it meant to be a woman in the times in which I was living. The writing was therapy coming from feelings of desperation, not from a broad intellectual need to understand the gender changes taking place in society as a result of the women's movement. The initial subject matter of what became a lifelong habit of writing therapy was related to my place in society, as a Christian woman, wife, and mother.

WHAT IS A WOMAN'S PLACE?

I was thirty-two years old when I wrote the first of numerous "memos to myself." The gist of the memo was: *Is there more to life than supporting a husband's and children's goals?* A handwritten note next to the date stated: "written following a particularly exasperating conversation with my husband."

> December 22, 1976 Re: Woman's place
> I've decided to begin to record some of the thoughts I have on the topics of marriage, women's rights, Christian women, working women, etc., because if I told any one of my friends, they would be shocked. My best friend, I guess, is my husband, and even though we have open communication in most areas, I have never been able to explain my feelings adequately to him in some of the areas mentioned above.
>
> Men have a way of putting women in their place by waiting until they are thinking rationally to discuss a subject. Women are known to be more emotional about most topics, and this serves as a scapegoat for men who are afraid of discussing in detail the topics their wives are so much in need of discussing.
>
> So, what communication is all about in so many marriages is to discuss openly the topics husbands feel comfortable in discussing. A marriage did work under these circumstances before the women's rights movement, working wives and mothers, and highly educated women. Now that we're more informed about our rights, women are coming up against frustration upon frustration that is, in my mind anyhow, frightening, depressing, and most likely unsolvable.
>
> Some of the frustrations I'm speaking of lie in the general area of a Christian woman's position in the home, the workforce, and the church. More specifically speaking, should a Christian

woman concentrate only on her husband's and children's achieve-
ments, making her major role one of supporting others? Or can
a Christian woman exercise her rights, as other women of the
times are doing, and have a career and a family life at the same
time?

This leads to more crucial questions. In a Christian family
where a woman works, who has the major responsibility for childcare and household management? Should a woman be expected
to hold down two full-time jobs (one a paid job and the other an
unpaid homemaker role), leaving her husband free to pursue his
own goals? How far should a woman bend to help her husband
achieve his goals, keeping in mind that her own goals may be unmet? Does a woman have the right to refuse to devote her entire
energies to meeting husband's and children's demands?

Why I decided at that particular time in my personal history to
record my thoughts has escaped me, but there were multiple things going on at the time that could have contributed to my search for answers.
First of all, my husband had an extremely busy schedule, which meant
he had no time to talk to me, and I had no friends in similar situations
with whom I could share my frustrations. Also, I was physically and
emotionally exhausted. My first memo should have discussed my weary
bones and failing health, but instead it reflected my lack of being able
to accomplish my personal goals. My earlier childhood and adolescent
dreams were attempting to surface. I was becoming dissatisfied with my
narrow, socially prescribed role.

Second, women's roles had become a controversial social issue.
It was the 1970s, and we had spent the prior fifteen years in two large
universities where hippies were conspicuously present. It was commonplace to see or hear about demonstrations and even riots. The world was
turned upside down—students were burning buildings and their bras,
and our men were dying daily in Vietnam. Most of this news was simply
background noise in my busy family life. I was too tired to pay much
attention to the world outside our community. But some of the unrest
registered and made me wonder how I fit into this new world that was
being created.

Third, the topic of women's roles was a social issue of great magnitude in our larger society, and I was attending a church where women
were basically silent, except for being allowed to teach children and sing
in the worship services. Perhaps the contrast between our conserva-

tive beliefs and society in the late 1960s and 1970s—in particular, the civil rights movement and the women's movement—was on my mind. Supposedly, women were being liberated by the women's movement that was underway. My values did not make sense in the new society that was taking shape. I believe I thought that most women in society had escaped the narrow confines of the family and were happily pursuing a life of their own, and that we Christian women were simply different. We were supposed to live our lives deliberately as we thought believers did in the early centuries of Christianity—at least, that is what I had been taught. I heard phrases like "back to the Bible," and "we are a New Testament Church," but contradictions were surfacing in my mind. I dared not speak those thoughts out loud.

In the 1960s and 1970s, articles about women's roles began to appear in the religious periodicals to which my husband subscribed. He later told me that he had been interested in what the Scriptures really said about women's roles since that time. But, we never actually discussed this, probably because we did not have time to talk about anything other than the children, household management, and our schedules, which were horrendous. Not having time to talk to the only person in my life with whom I really could talk about my ideas created an emptiness inside that was difficult to define. I would often lie in bed at night creating dialogues in my mind about things I needed to talk to someone about, but not bothering Gary because he was too busy studying.

In our own congregation in the mid 1970s, a prolonged study of elders had taken place, and one of the women in our congregation, who was a college professor, had written a treatise proclaiming her views on the topic. But, because of our stand on women remaining silent in the church, her husband had read her paper to the congregation. She sat quietly and listened. None of this made sense. It was the best argument I had heard, and I remember wishing I could present my ideas as well as she could. In this family, roles were reversed; the wife was the breadwinner and her husband the stay-at-home caretaker. They had four children and someone had to play that role. She had a flourishing career and he did not. They seemed quite happy with their chosen lifestyle, and I was perplexed and probably quite envious of a woman who did not have to go home from work and subsequently cook dinner and do the laundry. Her life offered the contrast necessary to trigger questions regarding our church's long-established interpretation of women's roles. Regardless of her competence and professional role in society, this woman, other than singing, remained silent in the worship service. My belief system was being challenged, and I had no place to turn for answers.

An additional factor that likely contributed to my frustration was the psychological urge to resolve some unfinished developmental issues from childhood and adolescence. At this point in my life, I came out of the cocoon I had been in since I left Colorado at age nineteen. I was attempting to become my own person, something most developmental psychologists now attribute to young adulthood. It is a healthy, necessary step toward an adult identity. Prior to my marriage, I had begun the process of individuation, becoming my own self.[7] But, when I married a minister, the way I lived my life was dictated by the church. In our church, nothing was written down, of course, about how a minister and his wife should live, but subtle comments and my observation of other Christians in our circle taught me swiftly how to behave. I complied, attempting to play the role of a perfect wife and mother.

As I struggled with my place in the world, I had no inkling of how the stage had been set in the 1950s for women who had worked outside the home during World War II to return exclusively to the nurturing role in which they were engaged prior to the war. My sheltered life on the farm, a limited education in a rural school, and a home without television and newspapers left me quite uninformed about larger society. I must have thought that all adult women everywhere were wives and mothers, that they were content with that role, and that I would follow suit. Any dissatisfaction felt was my fault; *there was something wrong with me.*

The reality of the 1950s and 1960s was that many American women were confused about their role in society and the home. According to historian William H. Chafe, "one of the byproducts of the war was a deepening sense of bewilderment among many American women over how to define their identity."[8] Women who had proven to themselves and others during World War II that they could make a difference outside the home were not as easily satisfied with being confined to a homemaker role. It was more than twenty years into my adulthood when I found how difficult the path to self-fulfillment had been for many women of those times, especially middle-class, well-educated women, a subculture of which I had become a part.[9] Wilma, the African American woman

---

7. See Levinson, *Seasons of a Man's Life*, *Seasons of a Woman's Life*, and "Women's Lives." See also Josselson, *Finding Herself.*

8. Chafe, *The American Woman*, 199.

9. For an in-depth discussion of these issues of women's identity, see Chafe, *The*

mentioned earlier, had a life story similar to mine in that our *subcultures* were dictating what women should do and be. We should be a support system for our husbands so they could provide well for the family. Women were expected to do whatever it took to make their husbands successful, and, in turn, their husbands would be good providers.

Therefore, the questions I was asking during the late 1970s were not all that unusual and would not have been shocking, as I assumed, had I discussed them with other women my age—though not every woman would have been helpful. Many women in our conservative church then, as today, honestly believed that women are better off in the home. And many, I am sure, are happy in that situation. In the late 1970s, a few Christian women began to question publicly, through articles and books, the role that women had unthinkingly followed for centuries. One book by Patricia Gundry is still in my library today, but then, I had no time to read. Gundry gently but compellingly approached the topic of biblical equality for women, going directly to the heart of the issue as she attempted to identify the problem:

> Many women in our churches feel like second-class Christians. The generic term *man* as used in the Bible repeatedly refers to mankind in general, but women are excluded from the application of many of these passages. It is as though an invisible hand rises to bar their way when they attempt to appropriate these passages for themselves.
>
> There have always been women who questioned the validity of their restricted service in the church. However, the citing of a few selected Bible verses or an argument based on "logic" was usually sufficient to silence all but the most persistent. If the questioner was not convinced, at least she kept her doubts to herself from then on.
>
> But women have been silent for so long that the church tends not to take them seriously now when they ask to be heard. They have so often sat quietly in classes with men, rarely commenting on any subject, that many men believe women have nothing to contribute. This is not true. Women talk freely among themselves, but in mixed groups, women somehow lose their confidence. They sense that their views are not considered to be of equal value with men's, so they remain quiet.[10]

American Woman; Hymowitz and Weissman, *A History of Women in America*; Gatlin, *American Women Since 1945*; and Coontz, *The Way We Really Are*.

10. Gundry, *Woman Be Free*, 9.

Gundry's statements made me first think of my mother, whom I know suffered in silence for many years. When she was in her seventies and eighties, she would discuss with me in our Sunday afternoon phone conversations what her minister had said that day, and occasionally she would carefully introduce the possibility that he might be wrong. I believe she never felt safe enough with anyone else to voice her own thoughts about the interpretation of Scripture. In spite of the fact that my mother was an extremely intelligent woman, decades of believing that women were to be silent stifled any confidence she might have had in her own thoughts. Suffering in silence to her meant keeping her mouth shut and minding her own business. To me, it meant grabbing pen and paper and writing my own thoughts about the subject, but never sharing them with others, and never knowing that, in another sector of society, academic women were beginning to put forth psychological theories explaining the outcomes of women's lack of voice in their own destinies.

Because of my overcommitment in the roles of wife, mother, and breadwinner, I did not have time to study and discuss in depth the contradictions I was beginning to notice. So, instead of seeking help through reading and counseling, I turned inward and continued to write, feeling alone and confused. I believed that the source of my problem revolved around the issue of a Christian woman's place in society, but this larger topic unfolded into a series of subordinate subjects that had to be addressed before I could formulate an answer to my initial question. That question was like the first domino in a set that, when slightly touched, initiated a chain reaction. The more I learned, the more questions I had about different aspects of women's lives.

SELFISH OR SELFLESS?

The first issue that filled my waking hours and often kept me from sleeping at night was whether a Christian woman with a husband and children could work outside the home for *personal gain or fulfillment*, or was it her lot in life to be only in a supportive role. I was nearing the end of seven years of employment to support our family while Gary was in school. Although I had some interesting jobs during those years, it became more difficult after each additional child was born to do anything more demanding than an eight-to-five secretarial job. Once Gary took a full-time position as a college teacher and I finally had a *choice* about whether to work or not, the issue was continually on my mind.

He wanted me to stay home and take care of the children, and I was well aware of the social expectations that I do so.

The question that must have been in my mind but not verbalized was: *Why could I work outside the home for the previous seven years when I had very small children, and now feel I should stay home?* My children needed me more the first few years of their lives. It appeared to be acceptable to work outside the home if you were doing it to promote your husband's goals, but not to pursue your own goals. Was the children's welfare the issue? Or was it really about gender inequality? Men had always held the dominant role in our society. In our case, the source of the inequality was not my husband. He was not trying to control me or keep me in my place. He was living out the role that men in his experience had unthinkingly followed. We were born and raised in a patriarchal society where men (usually elite, white men) were at the top, women next, and children at the bottom of the hierarchy. That is simply the way our social system worked, and little thought was given to the topic until the 1960s.[11]

In the 1970s, the academic debate over women's roles in society heated up, though it would be another ten years before I would be introduced to the literature being written about this topic. On one side, feminists claimed that women were equal and, therefore, should have equal opportunities and salaries in the workplace, the family, and in society in general.[12] On the opposing side, religious conservatives felt that women were more fulfilled as wives and mothers, and that being a good wife and mother meant that you must be a housewife, a full-time homemaker.[13] Somewhere in the middle were sociologists completing study after study to determine the effects of paid employment on the family.[14] Psychologists had begun to develop new frameworks for explaining gender roles in society. One author, Lillian Rubin, practically told my story. Rubin returned to school in 1963, the year I was married, but things had

11. See Johnson, "Patriarchy, the System."

12. See Mason, Czajka, and Arber, "Change." See also Epstein, *Woman's Place*; Feldberg and Glenn, "Male and Female"; Ferree, "Working-Class Jobs"; and Lopata and Thorne, "On the Term 'Sex Roles.'"

13. LaHaye, *The Spirit-Controlled Woman*; Hancock, *Love, Honor, and Be Free*; Olds, *The Mother who Works outside the Home.*

14. See Waite, "Working Wives"; Eriksen, Yancey, and Eriksen, "The Division of Family Roles"; Kanter, *Work and Family*; Oppenheimer, "The Sociology of Women's Economic Role"; and Pleck, "The Work-Family Role System."

not changed significantly by the time I returned to college twenty years later. Rereading portions of Rubin's book brought me to tears; I knew exactly how she felt. When a woman steps outside of her accepted role in society, or at least outside of the expectations of her own subculture, she becomes the butt of subtle criticism or silent scorn.

> When a woman embarks on such a course, her marriage often is under threat. But there was something else underlying these expressions of concern from people whose lives touched mine— something related to their own needs and their own resentments because I was no longer able to give them the time and attention they wanted. How often my brother's voice came across the miles of telephone line, anger masking his hurt: "Can I come to visit, or is my forty-year-old sister too busy doing her homework?" How often a friend responded to my inability to make a lunch date with: "Oh come on, surely you don't have to take it all *that* seriously." How often my mother sighed: "Some people are so lucky; their daughters come every Wednesday."
>
> It's true, as Marya Mannes says: "No one believes [a woman's] time to be sacred. A man at his desk in a room with a closed door is a man at work. A woman at a desk in any room is available." . . . A man, at work or at home, is the symbolic father, not to be disturbed—too busy, too preoccupied with the large tasks of life. A woman is the symbolic mother—always nurturant, always available—even when she is at work.[15]

In my subculture—the church—a woman was, and often still is, considered selfish, self-centered, or simply not a good Christian if she strays from the acceptable norms of the traditional wife and mother. Over the years, I have heard many ministers (all male, in my experience) talk about selfish people who do not follow the church's traditions, though we were led to believe that these traditions were the gospel truth, which the Bible said we must believe and do. However, what I have observed is that a person's interpretation of selfishness is gender-biased. Women are often kept in their place by being told they are selfish if they want their own needs fulfilled, yet men do not consider it selfishness when they focus on their needs, usually work. They can rationalize spending more time at work because they are providing for the family, but the same men often have wives who work outside the home. Even in the twenty-first century, a different standard remains for men and women

15. Rubin, *Women of a Certain Age*, 4.

regarding selfishness and needs fulfillment. Women are expected to be self-sacrificing, and if they vary from this, they are considered selfish. Men are expected to provide for the family and to concentrate on the public realm, so they are not expected to sacrifice for their wives and families. The fact that many women also help provide financially for the family has not changed the standard.

Among the most valuable theories to emerge from that era about the effects of cultural norms on a woman's psychological development were those published by Jean Baker Miller, who was attempting to redefine gender roles so that female traits were seen as positive and valuable for all of society.[16] She contrasted women's subordinate role in society, where they are considered submissive, caring, emotional, indecisive, serving, creative, passive, and dependent, with the male traits of aggressiveness, independence, strength, intelligence, leadership, autonomy, authority, power, and logic. I finally understood why I felt different: I felt my greatest strengths were those that had been assigned to males in our society. To survive seven years of working outside the home and managing a household of five required that I be aggressive, independent, strong, intelligent, and logical while also being caring and nurturing. I was continually torn between the traits of both the male and female models that had dominated our culture for centuries. However, in my own mind, the much more practical question of whether or not to work outside the home was at the forefront.

TO WORK OR NOT TO WORK: THAT IS THE QUESTION

Trying to answer this question took many hours of my time in late 1977 and early 1978, the year after Gary took a full-time position and I was free to be "just a housewife." The 1950s culture that had molded me conveyed to women the message that they were to be primarily wives and mothers, which translated into a hard life of service to others.[17] The bottom line message to white, middle-class Christian women was clear: *Women with children were not to be gainfully employed outside the home!* At the time, I did not have diverse enough life experience to realize that many women outside this narrow realm of white and middle-class had no choice but to work; otherwise, their families would not have survived. Very poor

16. Miller, *Toward a New Psychology of Women*. This book was one of the first to attempt to offer a theory of women's development that was not based on the male model of independence.

17. See Coontz, *The Way We Never Were* and *The Way We Really Are*.

and working-class women, especially African American women, had always contributed to the family income while maintaining a home. But, my childhood socialization had revolved around my mother, father, and brother, a few friends from school, and a small congregation of good, conservative Christians. The women were all housewives and all Caucasian. Somehow the idea of being a full-time wife and mother was equated with being a good Christian woman.

As far as I knew, my mother, a typical farmer's wife, followed without questioning the lifestyle of farmers' wives before her. She did what her mother and grandmother had done. Her generation was simply one of many cohorts of women who were dedicated housewives working alongside their husbands, doing whatever was required to survive. They were home with the children, but it was not an Ozzie-and-Harriet life they were leading. They worked extremely hard and were not rewarded with a paycheck. They took care of the unending household duties, nurtured the family (in small doses), and helped their husbands with the farming and outdoor chores. These chores included hoeing weeds in the hot sun, driving the tractor during planting or harvesting time, drawing water from a well or via a hand pump, and chasing pigs, cows, or chickens when they escaped from their pens.

Every week was very much the same. Monday was wash day. My mother drove the seven miles to town to an old-fashioned laundry where dirty clothes were put in a washer that had a tub for hot sudsy water and one for rinsing, and then they were run through a hand-turned wringer. After all the washing was completed, the heavy baskets of clothes were taken home, carried to the clothesline, and hung up to dry. Later that evening, they were sprinkled with water, rolled up, and placed in a basket, ready for ironing on Tuesday. (There were no permanent press fabrics in those days.) That left Wednesday through Saturday for baking, canning, gardening, sewing, cleaning, and a multitude of repetitious, mindless chores. Sunday was special. We went to church, had a large dinner, often with friends from church who had been invited to participate, and spent the afternoon socializing. Then, we went to church again.

The idea that women were physically or mentally weaker than men did not enter my mind as I observed my mother's daily workload. One of the most unsavory tasks I remember was the killing of chickens. She placed a squawking chicken on the ground, put a stick on its neck, and then pulled his head off. He flopped around the yard until totally dead, then, the smelly part came—dipping the dead chicken into boiling hot water so the feathers could be easily plucked. My job was to help with the plucking. Not one tiny feather could be missed. The slick insides were removed, and the chicken was cut into parts, washed, and put in the freezer. Later, he was pulled from the freezer, thawed, floured, and fried to a perfect crisp. We thought nothing of the killing process as we enjoyed the chicken along with mashed potatoes, homemade biscuits, and home-grown vegetables. It was rare to eat anything from a can, and microwaves did not exist.

Putting this image of my mother up against the image being cultivated in the 1950s would have been a major contradiction, *if* I had been exposed to what the social norms were. But, there were no opportunities for my friends and me to see what was going on in the rest of the world. We were basically in seclusion, and there was no discussion of activities outside our small farming community. Though some of our teachers tried to educate us, little of it stuck because we had no frame of reference to make sense of the information.

Needless to say, farm women in the 1950s seldom found time for themselves and it showed in their faces and demeanor. They were frequently too tired to be patient and caring mothers and wives, much less have the time to think about their own needs. And, *they did not have a choice* about whether to work or not work. They simply did not get paid for the work they did. I believe, though, their identity came more from their hard work—accomplishing daily an impossible "to do" list—than it did from their nurturing role. But I also think these women who had to work so hard to help their families survive did not necessarily want their daughters to have the same lifestyle when they were adults. Though they did not talk about it, our hardworking mothers wanted more for us: a life that was not so difficult and one that was more personally fulfilling. Regardless of what they wanted for their daughters, they were not equipped to prepare us for the outside world.

Ordinary women for generations before mine seldom had the opportunity to make a decision about whether to work or not work. If their families needed them to make money, women found a way to do it so that their families would be fed, warm, and properly clothed. But, they still were the primary caretakers of their families, and perhaps more importantly, their work was not considered an avenue for satisfying some deep need or giving them something meaningful to do with their lives. The work they did was for their families, not themselves. It was for survival.

Over the years, when my mother heard people (mainly me) complaining about not liking their work, she matter-of-factly stated "work is work; it is not supposed to be enjoyable."

Even when the times changed so that women had the choice to get an education and support their families as well as or better than men could, the leftover values from our female legacy told us that women were still primarily nurturers and homemakers. Subtle messages were conveyed to us: *to have careers and special, time-consuming interests of our own outside the home was unacceptable for a mother. It was selfish to think of our own needs!* The contradiction here is clear: My mother could work outside the home helping my dad make money and no one felt it was wrong, but it was selfish for me to work outside the home to make a better life for my family. Then, somehow between the 1950s of my childhood and the 1970s of my young adulthood, the rules seemed to have changed, but no one explained them to me. Much later, in the late 1990s, Stephanie Coontz revealed the inconsistencies and contradictions of the idealistic family of the 1950s,[18] but it was again too late to be of use to me.

So, the struggle began for me about the same time it began for other women in this country. Even though women for generations had managed to bring money into the family and simultaneously fulfill the nurturing role, it became a major social issue and a frequent cause for guilt among women who decided to have a *career* in the last half of the twentieth century. What exactly was the source of this guilt? Why was it such a struggle for women with children to make the decision to work outside the home once society had paved the way, through legislation, for women to compete in the workplace? It would be another ten years before I learned that what I was questioning in my own life was occurring throughout the Western world.

---

18. Coontz, in *The Way We Never Were* and *The Way We Really Are*, demonstrates how unrealistic and inaccurate our perceptions of the "perfect" 1950 families are. She makes the case that the 1950s family was a creation of society that emerged because of the dramatic events taking place in World War II and the ensuing Cold War. Government leaders felt that creating strong families was necessary for our society to survive in the postwar world.

2

Woman's Place and Social Change

WHEN I BEGAN IN the late 1970s to write memos, I was terribly confused about my role in society, but did not know why. I was not aware that living my life according to an outdated, socially subscribed female role in a world that was creating new norms for women was causing internal strife. I also was not aware that I had interpreted the source of my confusion too simplistically as an issue of whether I should work or not work, when there were much deeper, more complex issues being played out in my life. The topic of woman's place in the world, and, more specifically, my role in the family and church, was compounded by many things.

First, unlike generations of women before me, I was in the midst of a massive and radical change movement in our society and *I did have a choice*—but did not know *how* to make a decision for myself. I was an educated, competent, organized woman who had managed a family of five while working full-time, but I did not know how to think about myself, how to make decisions about what to do with my own life, because I had never been given *permission* to do so. There was something deep inside of me I could not label, which was prohibiting me from thinking about my own needs. I was paralyzed! It would be another twenty years before I encountered the phrase *permission to succeed* that helped to explain this. The initial phrase came from Sandy, one of my interviewees:

> I would be most interested in knowing who are the influences in successful women's lives who have given them permission to succeed in a society that still, by and large, does not recognize women as co-equal. That to me is what is really interesting.[1]

1. Sandy, a pseudonym, was a thirty-nine-year-old medical doctor and neonatal specialist. She was married and had a small child, but struggled continually to juggle her dual roles. This concept is discussed in more detail later in this book.

Sandy had received permission from her female legacy—a grandmother, mother, and female English teacher—to do something out of the ordinary with her life. She also was part of the first cohort of women to thrive in formerly male-dominated occupations. She was born in 1953, came of age during the women's movement, and consciously decided to follow a nontraditional pathway. Being from an earlier generation of women, those who were socialized to be only wives and mothers, I did not have this permission from society nor from my female legacy. Though both my mother and father encouraged me to obtain an education, they were not capable of seeing what my future could hold.

Because I did not understand the effect of my cohort and social change on my personal situation, I decided that the source of my unhappiness was our marital relationship. There were many overt signs of this. Gary's schedule was intense. We had moved to a university in the Southwest where he was teaching full-time and also working as a campus minister. In addition, he was trying to complete his doctoral dissertation during any spare time he could find. There was simply *no time for us.* For fifteen years, we had functioned like that, because we believed it was what most educated young couples of our time were doing. But I was at a point in my life when I needed something more. I had been trained to be a teacher, but had become a stay-at-home mom. I had unfulfilled needs of my own that I could not quite clarify, so I wanted him as a sounding board and confidant. I also wanted him to understand why I was unhappy. But he was afraid of my unhappiness and seemed to think that, if he ignored it, it would go away. My situation must have been duplicated thousands of times throughout the country as can be seen from women's writings that emerged in the 1980s.[2]

Focusing on the relationship with my husband as the source of my internal conflict was oversimplification. Theoretically, he was not opposed to my working outside the home, or pursuing more education, or whatever else I decided to do, but he wanted to be able to continue pursuing his own goals. What I did was pretty much up to me. But, something unspoken and even unlabeled was holding me back. About this time, a

---

2. Miller-McLemore (*Also a Mother*) was one of the few Christian writers able to make sense of the contradictions we discovered in the 1970s. She explained how narrow the interpretation was of changing women's roles in that decade. The women's movement represented an elite group of white, middle-class, educated women and did little for other women, especially the working class and women of color.

group of women social scientists, completely unknown to me and most other women in the country, began to research the developmental process of women in our society. The most eminent scholar, Carol Gilligan, published her first book, *In a Different Voice*, in 1982, a few years too late to help me understand the process in which I was in engaged.

Gilligan, a Harvard professor, began the study of women's development to demonstrate how existing theories of human development were actually only theories of *male* development, which defined men as separate and individuated. In other words, men were judged by their accomplishments and position in society, not by their relationships. Women were the opposite:

> [W]omen not only define themselves in a context of human relationship but also judge themselves in terms of their ability of care. Women's place in man's life cycle has been that of nurturer, caretaker, and helpmate, the weaver of those networks of relationships on which she in turn relies.[3]

When Freud and his contemporaries published their findings regarding human psychological issues, with a few rare exceptions, women were excluded. Freud's attempts to place women in his male model had resulted in more damage than good being done to women. Since women were not like men, he defined them as deficient, as being crippled by their emotions. Based on his own psychoanalysis of elite Victorian women, Freud created the term *hysteria* to explain the state in which many women were found. They were depressed and often hysterical when their emotions raged out of control. Women's nurturing role in society and their tendency to empathize and place high value on relationships were considered by Freud and his followers as negative traits, a weak position.

Gilligan was convinced that Freud and other psychoanalysts operating from his point of view were wrong. She relied on Nancy Chodorow's research to support her premise that women's focus on relationships was a strength, not a weakness. According to Chodorow, women naturally develop into caring, empathetic people because they identify more with their mothers: "feminine personality comes to define itself in relation and connection to other people more than masculine personality does."[4]

3. Gilligan, *In a Different Voice*, 17.
4. Chodorow, *The Reproduction of Mothering*, 43–44.

Gilligan clarified how girls "experience themselves as like their mothers . . . and emerge from this period with a basis for empathy built into their primary definition of self in a way that boys do not."[5]

With this theoretical background, Gilligan proceeded to test her hypothesis that the moral development of girls was not inferior to that of boys, as Lawrence Kohlberg had implied—just different.[6] Using Kohlberg's methodology, she interviewed young girls as well as adolescents and young adult women who were in the midst of making a decision regarding abortion. She arrived at the conclusion that females make moral decisions on the basis of relationships with others, not based on what is considered logical as boys and men do. Concluding that women are different from men, but not inferior, Gilligan continued with other Harvard researchers to engage young girls in her research process. In the late 1980s and early 1990s, she communicated her results on how females make the transition successfully from girlhood to womanhood:

> Privileged men often spoke as if they were not living in relation with others—as if they were autonomous or self governing, free to speak and move as they pleased. Women, in contrast, tended to speak of themselves as living in connection with others and yet described a relational crisis: a giving up of voice, an abandonment of self, for the sake of becoming a good woman and having relationships.[7]

Many girls unknowingly follow society's expectations for them and become what others want them to be; they have no voice of their own, but their dreams remain buried deep inside, waiting for something to trigger their reemergence.

> For over a century the edge of adolescence has been identified as a time of heightened psychological risk for girls. Girls at this time have been observed to lose their vitality, their resilience, their immunity to depression, their sense of themselves and their character.[8]

5. Gilligan, *In a Different Voice*, 9.

6. Kohlberg, known for his theory of moral development of young boys developed in the mid-twentieth century, concluded that boys' development was superior to girls' because they perceived what is morally right based on rational judgment rather than emotions.

7. Brown and Gilligan, *Meeting at the Crossroads*, 2.

8. Ibid.

In other words, women like me who had no clear personal identity when they reached adolescence were more likely to maintain their girlhood persona and, therefore, were more susceptible to depression and confusion. My interpretation of how Christian girls' and women's development was being impeded was confirmed by Gilligan and her colleagues as a psychological issue for women in general. I was interpreting my problems as personal and not as a normal part of women's developmental process in our society. Because I did not yet have the background to understand Gilligan's book, even if it had been available, it would have been overwhelming when I was in the midst of my search in 1976. I continued to interpret my situation more narrowly and blamed the church's teachings and my marital relationship as the sources of my unhappiness. I became more frustrated and, for the first time in my life, depressed.

RESPONSE TO FRUSTRATION

I continued to write because I had no one to talk to about my own needs. I had no close, lifelong friends and sisters. My mother lived in another state, and, even if she had been closer, she would not have understood my problem. My husband's primary work associate and his wife, much older than we and reasonable role models, had made it clear that a woman belonged at home, and I assumed their position was the popular opinion in that community. Actually, I assumed right. It was a conservative part of the country, isolated from the infusion of new social and political viewpoints, and it was still too early for career women to be commonplace. Any woman who broke away from that mold was considered selfish or self-centered at the least, and, by some, a sinner.

At the time they were written, my memos simply served as an emotional outlet, but as I interpret them now in light of what came before and after that period of my life, I realize how complex my life had become and how confused I was. What is immediately apparent from a close analysis of the memos is that *I could not resolve the issue I thought I was dealing with because I was not asking the right questions.* I believe now that one of the primary reasons for my restlessness was that I had never before (as an adult) had the luxury of thinking about myself because of my multiple roles of wife, mother, and breadwinner. When I tried to think about my future, there was nothing to think about. I was an empty shell. There was no cognitive framework around which to organize my thoughts. The cognitive structure built in childhood, which included my parents' and the church's teachings, was not adequate for interpreting the life events I was encountering. My restlessness and urge to write was my brain's natural technique for creating a new framework. I later learned from my academic studies that one of the primary means of modifying our cognitive structures is by comparing our life experiences with other people's experiences, comparing a specific time in life with a previous one, or comparing our current situation with what we thought we would be doing by this age. By completing this comparative analysis, we create our own personal narrative, making it possible for us to make sense of life. In memos, I recorded this process.

> September 1977
> Re: Just a housewife
>
> For the first time in my fourteen years of marriage, I am suddenly just a housewife. It leaves a strange, empty feeling inside when I must disclose this information (on such forms as my daughter's school entry form . . .), and I find myself justifying the position I hold.
>
> Why should I feel this way? I've worked hard through years of my husband's and my education. I've had three children, taking only enough time from my job to get my feet on the ground and to appear chipper. I've worked through night feedings . . . often getting as little as two or three hours of sleep because of a sick child. . . .
>
> Why should I feel guilty and useless now that I'm staying home and doing only the things that wives and mothers have been doing for centuries—washing everything as soon as it gets dirty, . . . picking up toys and stashing them in a place convenient for the kids to pull them down again, . . . being a chauffeur . . . ?
>
> Why am I so bored? Why do I feel like going to bed at 8:30 since I can't think of anything else to do? I've read every book in the house, playing the piano might wake the baby, watching TV doesn't appeal to me unless I have a lot of laundry to fold or mending to do, and I did that earlier in the day.
>
> I've tried in my most rational moments to analyze this feeling of frustration and depression that has come over me in the past few weeks, to draw some conclusion about my situation, and to plan moves for overcoming this maddening problem.
>
> My first strategy is to continually remind myself of what it was like when I was a hardworking, gainfully employed mother of three young children, and to compare some of the worse situations then to my present situation. One of the first things that come to mind is the trauma of losing and then selecting a new

babysitter. . . . I'll never forget the horrible moods I got in when I had to select a new one. At least, now that I'm "just a housewife," I don't have this problem.

Another thing I must remind myself of now that I'm bored is how very, very tired I was every evening while working outside the home, which meant that my prime time on weekdays was spent with outsiders, people I worked with, while the only time I had to spend with my family was when I was too tired to enjoy them. I must not forget the headaches that came so often then, so seldom now, and what about the many times I fell asleep on the couch before 9:00 p.m. on Friday nights because I had let down my mental reserve that kept me going all week?

Making this comparison between the past fourteen years and the one I've just begun still doesn't ease entirely the feeling that something is amiss in my life. What I think is the key problem here is the lack of contact with other people with similar interests and backgrounds. . . .

From this self-analysis, I have concluded that one of the most noticeable changes in me is one of self-esteem. When I was a working woman, I was conscientious; consequently, I received a number of compliments from people with whom I worked. . . . This feeling of self-worth kept me going through extremely exhausting and trying circumstances, while now it takes very little to get me into a state of depression or physical tiredness, which must be the consequence of my mental state.

Although not in perfect form, my writing had become therapy for me. I enacted both the therapist and the client roles, but, as I learned many years later from rereading my memos, my solutions were temporary. Some fragmented thoughts would fall into place only to be replaced with new ones. The depression and anxiety kept returning.

The memo above was written about one month after we moved from Iowa to the Southwest. It was three months before I wrote again, but I remember during that time taking up several hobbies, including quilting, to keep myself busy. I was doing what my mother enjoyed doing in her spare time because I had never cultivated interests of my own other than reading and playing the piano. I was trying hard to be the perfect wife and mother. My house was clean by 9:00 a.m., so I spent many hours each day with our youngest son, who was a toddler. I put him on the back of my bicycle and we explored the small town where we lived.

During those four months, we made friends with a young couple about our age. She had just begun to work outside the home, and they, unlike us, had few money problems. I was depressed because I was bored and we needed my income. One visit triggered another memo.

> December 11, 1977
> Re: To work or not to work
> Several years ago, my husband and I determined that never would both of us work full-time at the same time, because we did not want to fall into the trap that so many young married couples do: that of getting used to two incomes and not being able to do without one of them. After a number of years of higher education, when we both worked part-time, or I worked full-time while my husband worked part-time, . . . we are now living like the typical young married couple. . . . My husband holds down a full-time teaching position, and I am staying at home with the children and doing my duty as wife and mother.
>
> The problem with this arrangement is we are continually in difficult financial straits. And the spells of depression that were so common a few months ago were often brought on by the fact that I was well educated, quite experienced, and capable of getting out and going to work to help supplement our income, and yet we had made our promise to each other—and besides, didn't our children deserve some time with their mother?
>
> Seeing our friends "getting so far ahead" of us in the material things of life was quite difficult for me to digest at the time. But, after a few months of a relatively peaceful household, being available when my children need me, getting things done that I had left off for years, I can finally visit our friends and feel not in the least bit jealous or depressed by the things they have that we do not have. I think it was the tired look on their faces that really brought the issue home to me. I had looked like that for so long and knew exactly what she must have felt like when we left for home, and she had a number of undone chores around home. And yet, she had to face going to work tomorrow morning and likely never finding the time to catch up at home.

This memo defined the problem, or at least the problem as I interpreted it at the time, and then jumped to a solution. Part of the resolution was to remind myself of the difficult time I had when juggling work and family, and also to remind myself of our family values: rearing children who had access to their parents. I also began here a practice that continued for years: writing a *happy ending* to many of my memos.

It was a form of a solution, but a very short-term one. It helped me with the depression of having my life on hold by delaying the gratification to another time, and, in the meantime, I gave myself an activity to keep me going until the gratification was possible. These two techniques—writing happy endings and delaying gratifications—were, at the time, healthy coping strategies that gave me the time necessary to process what was going on in my life.

Finally, through a lot of rationalizing and self-talk in memos, I seemed to come to terms with not working outside the home. Gary and I agreed it was best, and I was finding ways to adapt. But it turned out to be a fleeting contentment. I made it through the holidays and into February before another memo was written. This one showed how serious the issue of whether to work or not to work had become for me. I could not quit thinking about it, probably because we were struggling financially, and I had always been the one to pull us out of a financial bind, since Gary's job and school demands made it impossible for him. This memo was an attempt to analyze the issue academically and unemotionally.

> February 1, 1978
> Re: Working outside the home
> For years, I have been listening to sociologists, religious leaders, economists, marriage counselors, and knowledgeable laypersons discussing the pros and cons of working mothers and what it has done to our society, primarily our children. I have tried to keep an open mind on the subject, since I am sincerely concerned about my own children and other children; however, I have never felt that the working mother has received fair representation.
>
> For instance, how often do you hear discussed the effects that gainful employment has on the mother herself as a person, how working outside the home has positively influenced her relationship with her husband, how it affects the way she feels about herself, and, consequently, how she treats others? It is true that a woman has a great responsibility and obligation to rear her children in the best way possible, but does that automatically mean she should spend twenty-four hours a day at home with her family or involved in activities that will directly benefit them? *Must she sacrifice her own interests to the point that she has no self-esteem left?*

Following this introduction, I dedicated several paragraphs to explaining to my imaginary audience the beneficial effects of working outside the home. I assumed staying in the workforce was a "near guarantee" that you could be employed once your children left home. I suppose I had heard about the empty-nest syndrome, where women became unhappy or bored with their role and decided to go to school or work. I also felt that working outside the home had motivated me to do the best I could as a homemaker, because I had always done that on the job. In other words, I was organized and efficient, accomplishing a lot in a short time period so I could spend more time on the important things in life, such as quality time with the children. I began to think about what kind of person I would have been had I not worked outside the home for so many years.

> I would likely have been the type of wife who avoided social activities because she had no confidence in herself. My entire life would have been wrapped up in what my husband and children were doing at the time. I would have continually worried that I wasn't pleasing my husband (and, on the other hand, my husband would have learned to expect me to be the "traditional homemaker" who met his every need without questioning).
>
> Since, in all fourteen of the years that I have been married, I have been involved either in going to school or working, my husband and I have worked out (and it wasn't easy to reach that point) a relationship that is as close to 50/50 as any I've seen. We are both very considerate of the other's needs and time pressures.
>
> Each of us easily recognizes when the other is in need of some special understanding and knows that it is "my turn" to take an overload of housework, child care, shopping, etc., to relieve the other of unnecessary pressure. I doubt that my husband ever takes me for granted, and vice versa, because we have learned through several years of tight schedules and sharing duties that, regardless of what the other is doing, it is important to him/her and should be acknowledged.

As usual, I had a happy ending, though it was not even close to reality. Our marriage was becoming more lopsided. I was quite simply "Gary's wife." As a wife, I helped him in his work as a campus minister and served as the children's support system, but I had *no separate identity*. At that time, I was not familiar with the term *identity* and had no idea how psychologically damaging it was not to have a clear personal identity. The problem I was having was similar to what Betty Freidan wrote about in the 1960s. Her well-known book, *The Feminine Mystique*, was published in 1963, the year I got married, and I would not, at the time, have been able to relate to her "problem with no name." By 1978, it would have made sense, but I had heard through the Christian grapevine that Freidan was a radical, and, therefore, I did not consider her book worth reading.[9]

During the 1970s, ministers throughout the country were speaking out against the women's movement, glorifying women's traditional role, and, whether intentionally or not, making women like me feel more guilty about working outside the home:

> A voice needs to be raised for wifehood—woman created by God so man would not be alone. A voice needs to be raised for motherhood—woman who has given us life, nurtured us in youth, and has been a dominant influence on everything we are.[10]

His thesis was that woman is not inferior, she is equal and powerful, but she draws her power from submission: "This is the power Jesus demonstrated on the cross. He yielded in suffering and obedience. Through this he received exalted power. Likewise, the very submissiveness of woman has a mighty power"[11] He claimed that a "godly woman is eloquent by her quietness . . . by possessing a meek and quiet spirit."[12] He summarized his thesis by saying, "the glory of God's woman is to be found in three things: her power of submission, her beauty in modesty, and her eloquence of quietness."[13] The logical outcome for a woman like me who was not well-informed in the Scriptures was to buy into his argument, decide I was not a godly woman, and then to feel guilty.

Also fueling the guilt among Christian women of the times was Neil Lightfoot, who published a book in 1978 on the role of women in the church. After a brief history lesson on how women had attempted to enter seminaries and become preachers in the nineteenth century, he segued to the twentieth century movement that was, he thought, doing more damage:

> I think it is fair to say that much of the recent interest on woman and the church is due to the Women's Liberation Movement. In no sense can this be termed a "Christian" movement. Women's

9. When I read the book in the 1980s, I found it to be far from the radical description I had received twenty years earlier.

10. Jividen, *Glorious Woman*, 148.

11. Ibid., 150.

12. Ibid., 151.

13. Ibid.

Lib is confessedly a revolutionary movement. It seeks to uproot marriage and the family and all conventional male-female
relationships. It aims at power and rule by the sheer weight of
female numbers and has spawned radical feminist groups,
such as WRAP (Women's Radical Action Project) and WITCH
(Women's International Terrorist Conspiracy from Hell). Clearly,
Women's Lib is a secular movement with a secular cause, guided
by principles many of which are patently non-Christian and anti-
Christian.[14]

Most Christian women of the times would have no frame of reference to recognize Lightfoot's technique of indicting an entire movement by citing extreme examples. Perhaps the movement could be
labeled revolutionary, but Jesus' movement in the first century was also
revolutionary. But, after considerable study of the women's movement
many years later, I found no references to the radical organizations he
was referencing, and the women's movement mission was not to "uproot
marriage and the family." But his book, along with many similar articles
on the subject, served his purpose of keeping Christian women in their
proper places.

During this period, probably because I felt guilty and inadequate, I
would not admit to myself or to others that my marriage was not good. I
wore a pleasant mask, and no one would guess that I was not the perfect
wife and mother happy with my situation. But, if my life were as rosy
as I presented it, why did I continue to write memos that so noticeably
showed my confused state and did not help resolve the issue? I felt I
had no choice: My husband and children needed me at home, and my
upbringing and religious subculture, the church, was telling me I would
be a bad mother if I worked outside the home. *I would be selfish and
materialistic.* My technique of writing happy endings was an attempt to
convince myself that I wanted to do what everyone else expected me to
do. It was a survival technique, but would not necessarily be a psychologically healthy one if, over a long period of time, I could not resolve
any of the issues. Assuming a face that was not authentic could, over
time, manifest itself in emotional and physical health issues.[15] Although
I was thirty-four years old and had juggled work/family like a profes-

14. Lightfoot, *The Role of Women*, 8.

15. In the 1990s, when I conducted my own research on professional women,
I discovered how important authenticity is to women in midlife. Living your life by
someone else's prescription prevents one from becoming authentic.

sional, I had been successfully trained to do, without questioning, what others expected of me.

On April 14, 1978, I wrote the last memo on the subject of working outside the home, because a perfect temporary solution was presented— one that allowed me to be at home when the children were, and yet make a little extra money. I was offered a part-time teaching position at the university where my husband taught. It gave me, for one year, a good option that allowed me the time I needed for my baby to become a preschooler, when he would be eligible for the university's daycare center.

What I did not know at the time was that my year of introspection had triggered an internal search for identity and meaning that would not be resolved for many years. The conflict between work and family obligations and personal needs fulfillment was just beginning. And, questioning the status quo in organizations, at work, and in church became a way of life for me that did not subside for many years. I was engaged in a long identity-clarification process that I later learned from my academic studies was actually a good thing. I was becoming the authentic person I was intended to become. The journey required much introspection and clarification of the internal conflicts fueled by contradictions between my upbringing in the church and the chaos of our changing society. I felt out of sync with the direction society was taking, making me restless and continually in search of answers.

3

Feeling Out of Sync with the Times

> Identity confusion . . . ongoing for a good while. The inner and
> outer are not in sync. . . . I have some strong things going on
> inside. . . . Innermost feelings are not approached or revealed.
> And I'm just beginning to find those.[1]

AFTER THE SERIES OF memos on whether to work or not, I began
the next series on finding my niche. Still unaware of what was happening in society and without a clue of what I was really doing, I began
a search for meaning: something that would make me feel like the life I
was living was worthwhile. Even though women in my family for generations had been primarily wives and mothers, for some reason, it was
not enough for me.

> November 3, 1978
> Re: In search of a niche
>   It's one of those cold, rainy evenings just made for a fireplace
> and a cup of soup, and it's a perfect time to think upon memories,
> ideals, future goals, and more: specifically, what's my place in this
> world.
>   Regardless of how hard I try, I cannot be content with a "nor-
> mal" life where I play the roles of wife, mother, homemaker, and
> partial breadwinner. That's not enough. I want to be somebody!
> Not a politician or a politician's wife, not wealthy, not a leader of
> a cause, not the most beautiful, most talented, nor the smartest—
> just somebody important, someone who contributes positively
> to her environment, and yet that isn't enough. Any law-abiding
> citizen fits that category.
>   I know that, hidden somewhere beneath those socially ac-
> cepted behaviors that I dutifully exhibit, there is a job just wait-

1. Thirty-five-year-old woman interviewed in 1992.

35

ing for me to tackle it. It is a problem that no one else can solve as well as I can. It is a job that allows me to fulfill my creative needs, utilizes my organizational and motivational skills, and yet not too demanding so the family is neglected. It permits me to be feminine, to use my brain, and to compete with men and women on an equal basis. It must not be so overpowering that I am never free from its clutches.

Throughout the next few months after the memo above was written, I became extremely anxious and restless. I was teaching part-time, thoroughly enjoying my work, but there was something else causing the discontent. Though I was unaware of it, *I was in the beginning of a major life crisis involving much deeper issues than simply whether I would work or not.* I would leave the children with Gary and go for long walks, trying to think clearly about my life. But I could not sort the tangled web of thoughts into any kind of organized structure that made sense. I felt like my head was going to explode from the inability to label the problem.

A LIFE REVIEW

After several months of anxiety, I reached a point where I felt I had to do a life review, an analysis of my life from childhood to the present time to try to understand what was wrong with me. It never entered my mind that I needed a therapist, because that was simply not acceptable in my circle of acquaintances. In fact, I had heard a minister in our church discuss how unnecessary counselors were for Christians. According to him, all we needed to do was read the Bible and pray. But it wasn't working for me, so I became my own therapist that Sunday afternoon.

> January 3, 1979
> Re: My life review
>
> If ever I am to understand exactly what "makes me tick," I believe I must go back to the beginning of my memories and attempt to relate my early childhood experiences to the feelings of fear, unrest, and confusion I'm having today and have had for many months now. Maybe the image I have had of myself all along (for thirty-four years now) isn't the real me; it could be simply what I like to think I am and has no relation at all to what I actually am deep inside.

In a search for the source of my anxiety, I wrote pages of rather insignificant events from childhood. I concluded that I had a fairly normal childhood and that nothing traumatic had happened to make me the confused, unsettled person I had become. The problem appeared to have begun after high school when I enrolled in a small, church-supported college. There, my earlier dreams of doing something worthwhile with my life had faded.

> I had one goal: to get out of that little town (where I was raised), do something exciting with my life, and definitely not to marry young and settle down having children immediately out of school like so many of my friends. I was not to marry until I was twenty-six, had my own car and piano, and had spent some years in India or some other disadvantaged country doing good deeds. . . .
> My first mistake was choosing a small, Christian-oriented school, where nearly everyone's goal was to find a spouse, and in most cases, as soon as possible. Before this time, I had given little thought to marriage, had dated very little because about the only things boys ever invited me to were forbidden by my parents (dances mainly), and I planned several years of independence before marriage.
> Without really knowing what was happening, I was swept into the social life of a small college and before long was "going steady" with a senior (every freshman's dream). Little did I know that this particular senior was thinking from the beginning of finding a mate to settle down with (for a lifetime). All his friends had already fallen into the trap, and he was feeling the urge to settle down also.

Later, after I finished my life review essay, I asked a friend to read it and help me understand myself. This person was someone I felt I could trust with my secret unhappiness because he was a good listener and, more importantly, open about his own problems. I think it was important that he was not "perfect," because I perceived my husband as being *the perfect Christian*. When this friend read my life story, he underlined the word *trap* in red. I had not even realized the significance of that word, but it was a good description of how I was feeling.

> Up to this point, I guess I was never really allowed to make a decision about my life, though I fancied that I was quite independent. It has taken me years to figure out exactly what did happen (if I even know yet). How did my plans get so messed up? Why did I allow "doing the 'in' thing" to interrupt and even cancel out my dreams to do something really big with my life? I know I had the ability, enough brains, and the drive to succeed in about any-

thing I tried, but somehow I was never allowed to try. I seemed to simply drag along and let other people completely control my life, without even knowing what they were doing.

My mother wanted me to be a home economics teacher, so I majored in home economics without another thought. My brother came along and said he thought I wouldn't enjoy all that chemistry (I hated it in high school), so why didn't I go into music? So, I changed my major again.

My brother introduced me to Gary, the senior who so radically changed my plans, so I went along with him and began dating quite steadily within a few weeks, only one time breaking away for a date with another boy, who definitely wasn't pushy enough to try to break up a "budding romance."

Three months later (at Christmastime), much to my surprise, Gary asked me to marry him, and I thought I had to make a decision right then. I liked him too much to say no. I simply never thought through rationally what I was doing. (I was eighteen years old.) Someone else had always done that for me, and under pressure is not a good time to learn how to make decisions, how to say no. . . .

June arrived, and I headed back to Colorado to collapse for a month while Gary took off for a three-month job in Canada. All my friends back home were so excited about my marriage, and I had no choice but to begin wedding plans, though my mother took care of most of that. I was busy trying to figure out how I was going to support a husband through a master's degree, which was Gary's next step in his life's design.

It seems ludicrous now that, at age 18, I made without much thought one of the most important life decisions I was ever to make. I went from doing what my mother and father said to what my husband expected, and, more important but subtle, what the church, interpreted by individual Christian women, wanted of a young, soon-to-be minister's wife. I was not consciously aware of any of these traditions and expectations. I was floating along, basically doing what women in my family had always done, keeping the house spotless, cooking from scratch, and, in addition, trying to make a living for our family.

The first fifteen years of marriage had been totally absorbed by Gary's plans. His plan, though I am sure he discussed it with me, was all about his education, his career, and his approach to serving God. It was not a self-centered act on Gary's part because I had no plans for my life. I had no role models, other than my mother, her sisters, my grandmother, and a few farm wives who were friends of my mother. The only vague thought in my mind regarding my future was that I needed an education, and that must have been planted by my parents. Many young men of their generation lost their lives in World War II, so they felt I needed an education as an insurance policy in case I had to work to support myself. I continued on that Sunday in January 1979 trying to find my niche:

> Fifteen years later, I am still trying to find that dream job that will make me feel like I'm worth something, that my purpose on this earth was not just to support a husband and children, but that there is something I can do better than anyone else that will not only fulfill my inner needs, but at the same time, help mankind in some way. I have no desire to be a "very important" person. . . . I want a simple yet challenging job working with people, and yet I can't clear the cobwebs from my mind enough to clarify exactly what "my thing" is. Why can't I accomplish such a task when I clearly have leadership abilities, the ability to make decisions, and the desire to do something worthwhile with my life?

The remainder of my writing that day was an attempt to understand myself. Obviously something was wrong with me. I looked at all my faults, the "barriers in the way of my understanding myself." I had trouble relating to people: "I find normal people uninteresting." I did not like being with strangers, being in crowds, so assumed I was basically unfriendly: "Could this possibly go back to the fact that I spent the majority of my childhood alone, doing my own thing, and seldom playing with other children?"

I also questioned my ability to truly love anyone because I could not communicate my feelings. And, I was disturbed because I enjoyed having male friends; I found them more interesting than females. Basically, I believed they were more accepting of me than women. I concluded, because I had lost my father in a car accident when I was twenty-three, I liked to be around men who were like him. I completed the life review, but came to no conclusions. I quit abruptly with a short paragraph that gave me an assignment:

> Obviously, I'm not a very good psychiatrist, and hope that I am giving too much attention to this problem, that it isn't really as big of a problem as I imagine it is. Somehow I must find out, though, what the "real me" is.

That last statement, as usual, gave me an assignment, which served the purpose of keeping my mind busy and my emotions in control. From the writing, I identified at least a portion of my problem: Who was I really? This is an identity question. I had no identity of my own. I was only a wife and mother, a Christian woman with a duty to fulfill. Had I known even a little about the history of women for the past two thousand years, I would have felt some comfort from the fact that I was quite similar to other women throughout recorded history.

SEARCH FOR THE "REAL ME"

When women struggle to make any life decision, such as whether to work outside the home or dedicate all their energies to the family, I believe there are unconscious elements at work, including hidden messages that have been buried since childhood, yet still haunt us. For many years, I was untrusting of all psychologists, counselors, and psychotherapists, but occasionally ran across writings that helped me appreciate the insights of professionals in this field. Many have a great deal to offer people who are frustrated, restless, or depressed. In the past thirty years, psychotherapists who have written about and published what they have learned from their female patients have laid the groundwork for us to begin to understand women's development. One of the first helpful psychoanalysts I discovered was Roger Gould, who began writing in the late 1970s.[2] Gould, who based his work on Carl Jung's theories,[3] referred to the hidden messages that adults struggle with as *childhood consciousness*.

> To brew up an adult, it seems that some leftover childhood must be mixed in; a little unfinished business from the past periodically intrudes on our adult life, confusing our relationships and disturbing our sense of self. I call this unfinished business childhood consciousness. Every time we feel anxious, depressed, afraid, inadequate or inferior and say to ourselves, "There's no good reason to feel this way," childhood consciousness has invaded our adult consciousness. We won't outgrow it, and we can't will it away. To achieve adult consciousness we must overcome childhood consciousness.[4]

2. Gould, *Transformations*; see also Gould, "Transformations during Early and Middle Adult Years."

3. Carl Jung has written volumes on the unconscious, including *The Undiscovered Self* and *Memories, Dreams, Reflections*.

4. Gould, *Transformations*, 17.

Once I discovered Gould's writings, I read and reread them until the pages fell out of the book because his words were the only ones that addressed what was happening to me. There was a deep, inner voice paralyzing me. I could not do what I wanted to do with my life because I had not been given permission to break away from the traditional woman's mold. I was operating from unconscious messages or rules of behavior, ones I could not identity at the time. At times, I felt I was going crazy because I could not formulate coherent thoughts. Life did not make sense.

Gould's work addressed both men and women, so I used his theory to analyze women's development, in particular, my own:

> In the process of discovering who she is, a woman frequently destroys relationships, usually those between herself and her children and between herself and her husband. These relationships in many cases may be hindering the development of the self, but, in other cases, the unconscious self coming back from childhood may be the main offender. It leaves the woman with a feeling of desperation. She is confused, angry, unfulfilled, and running out of time; she is nearly midlife, but no one seems to understand her, not even those who have been close to her for years.[5]

The issue that I and numerous other women like me were addressing in the 1970s, and which is still being resolved among young wives and mothers, is not simply whether or not to work outside the home, but how to find meaningful work around family obligations. For some, meaningful work may not be paid employment; for others, a second paycheck may be necessary to keep the family afloat financially. And, to make it more difficult, what is meaningful to one person may not be for another. Each woman has to define for herself what makes her life worthwhile. Once a woman has determined just what she wants, she is more likely to make it happen. But, this entire process requires energy and time that is seldom available to women with children.

Beginning to find the "real me" was an overwhelming chore without more knowledge in a variety of fields. Along with history, I needed to know about the effect of changing social roles on personal development, but had little sociological foundation from which to proceed. I did not know how significant it was that the masses of American women finally had an opportunity to have a career and a family, and that this had never been possible in the past.

---

5. Written in 1983 for a graduate class in human development.

In the late 1970s, I was offered a part-time teaching job at the university where my husband was teaching, so I jumped into the academic literature to prepare for my classes: child development and marriage and family. I became totally absorbed by what I was reading, spending nearly forty hours per week in what was supposed to be a part-time job. Although I did not realize it, this was a healthy way to begin the process of finding my personal identity. I was studying the normal developmental process of children, which led me to think of my own development and to wonder what went wrong in my childhood or adolescence to make me so confused in adulthood.

FINDING PARTIAL ANSWERS

My attempt at self-therapy through reading and writing was a good idea, but not initially successful because I needed feedback and support from others who either knew more about what was happening to me or had resolved similar crises. I had no idea at the time that what I was experiencing was fairly normal for someone my age who had not truly experienced and resolved the adolescent crisis, which should, according to Erik Erikson, end with the emergence of a clear personal identity.[6]

Instead of getting married at age nineteen and becoming a support system for others, I needed to grow up, separating from my family of origin and discovering my own unique self. I needed to create an identity of my own based on my childhood experiences and dreams and the value system that had evolved from these experiences.[7] As it happened, I adopted for myself a group identity (Christian woman) created by men and women who had mindsets, personalities, and a value system that had little connection with the "real me." I had found an identity dictated by others. Even though I had been reared in a Christian home, there were few dictates regarding what Christians "do." I was quite unaware of what it meant to belong to a group that interpreted the Scriptures in such a way that little individual freedom was allowed. This contradicted my childhood on the farm with nearly total freedom regarding how I spent my time (after chores were done). Because of that freedom, I never succumbed to peer pressure and had no clear group identity. According to lifespan experts, Erikson in particular, acquiring a group identity is a

6. Erikson, *Identity: Youth and Crisis*.
7. Ibid.

developmental task of early adolescence, approximately ages twelve to eighteen.[8] At age nineteen, however, I was just beginning to learn the rules of the Christian subgroup to which I was associated when abruptly I was required, because of my early marriage, to assume an adult role. Therefore, I was forced to become an adult before resolving the adolescent stage.

What finally triggered the search to find my true self? I believe now that it had much to do with the fact that we lived in a large Midwestern university town during chaotic times in our society. There was drastic social change all around us and, in typical graduate student style, we discussed all the ills and advancements of our society. The fact that I began questioning and writing in the mid 1970s is a telltale sign that I was somewhat aware of what was going on in society, in spite of my busy schedule. Then, when we relocated to the Southwest where Christian values were more conservative, the contrast caused me to question my earlier commitment to the church to which we belonged.

Even though I felt at times during those traumatic years that I was losing my mind, what was happening psychologically was healthy: I was being given another chance to find myself and create a life that flowed directly from my real self, the person I was meant to be. Though I could not recognize the signs, the terrible feelings of restlessness and uncertainty were warnings that my life needed to be redirected. My quest for a niche of my own, coupled with problems in my marriage and a lackluster spiritual life, were clues that I needed some hard work on myself. Through little fault of my own, my system was malfunctioning. The most visible symptom, though not the underlying cause, was discontent with my marriage.

8. Ibid.

4

Questioning My Marriage

I N NEARLY THIRTY YEARS of writing memos, there were very few that dealt with my marriage and relationship with my husband. But, since I wrote memos primarily when I was trying to solve a problem or clear my head of some frustration, one occasionally related to my dissatisfaction with my marriage.

Although I could not describe them at the time, the problems in our marriage were not as much related to my husband himself as they were to his choice of career, the amount of time it took away from the family, and the necessity that I be closely involved in his work, and therefore, not have time to pursue my own work. For many years, he was a campus minister and, *without consciously choosing it*, I was his partner in the ministry. This meant that I had to sacrifice any personal goals I had. Since a person's goals stem from his or her entire life experiences and role models from early childhood on, it is totally unreasonable to expect one person to assume the goals of another without some serious questioning and conscious decision making. But women, and especially Christian women, have been asked to do that for centuries.

One of the root causes of my discontent and inability to meet my own goals was the fact that the needs of my family were so great, and I felt guilty if I did too much for myself. My nurturing mindset was not that unusual for women of my generation. Those of us born before, during, or immediately after World War II and socialized to believe that woman's place is in the home could not automatically throw away our beliefs and adopt those of the changing society. Most of us did not apply the women's movement to our own situations because we were already engrossed subconsciously in a lifestyle that prevented us from taking care of our own needs first. Therefore, marriage was not necessarily blissful, but it was what it had always been for women in our female legacy.

Our legacy told us that "we made our beds, now lie in them." I can visualize my grandmother saying these very words. We had committed ourselves to a marriage and we should stay with it regardless of how unhappy we were. Our wedding vows clearly stated that we would "cherish and obey" our husbands for the rest of our lives. With that foundation, the job at hand was to make our marriages work, and, as far as I know, most women of my cohort did. But, it was extremely difficult in my case because I had strong personal goals; perhaps I was even ambitious (though we women do not like to discuss this topic.)[1] Beginning in 1979, I finally got the courage to write about my relationship with my husband.

> Another question that has been haunting me lately is: Why am I able to tell a person other than my husband about my innermost feelings, and yet cannot communicate these to him? Is it because I know what he expects of me, and that he will disapprove of me because of these feelings I have? Is it because I feel if I confide in him he will lose confidence in me? . . .
>
> One psychologist said that the inability to show love to the person closest to you will result in turning your affections to someone or something else: a child, animal, music, another person outside the family. Not being able to communicate and express yourself in a normal, everyday situation causes emotions to build up so much inside that they are easily unloaded when an understanding person comes along.

During this turbulent period, I had turned obsessively to the writing of and listening to music. In one song, I pleaded with God for answers. Each verse, which was my voice questioning the life I was living, had a responding verse, an answer from God. His responses told me what he wanted me to do with my life. My music was an attempt to discover my unique purpose in life, what talents I was supposed to use. I believe I was already aware that I was different from other Christians with whom I associated, or, more accurately, I was at least different from what I *perceived* other Christian women to be. Because of my attempts to become what other people wanted me to be, my spirituality was deeply

---

1. See Fels, *Necessary Dreams*, for a thorough discussion of how women interpret the word "ambition" as a negative trait.

buried. Music seemed to be the only medium through which I could reach God. It gave me temporary relief and confirmation that my life was basically on the right path. God was simply not giving me a detailed to-do list. What exactly I was to do with my life was still unknown, but at least I felt some type of a connection with God, something that was too often not present. It was another form of a happy ending, giving me time to figure out my next move.

I felt at times that I was competing with God, since Gary was a minister. When I would finally become frustrated enough to say what I felt, he was afraid to acknowledge my feelings. He felt I was too emotional and that we should wait until I could be more rational to discuss my feelings. Without realizing what he was doing, he was quietly putting me down, belittling what I thought was important.

Often my reaction to our discussions made me feel there was something wrong with *me*, not our marriage. I was too emotional or unstable; I was the problem and needed to be fixed. I was unhappy in my marriage and dissatisfied with my lack of career focus. I was spending most of my spare time helping Gary with his job and picking up the slack at home (pulling weeds, gardening, taking care of the children, doing the laundry, cooking for the family and student activities) to allow him the time necessary to study for the classes he was teaching and to write his dissertation.

Once I began working full-time outside the home again, I gave up trying to make Gary understand my needs. Though I continued to be involved in social activities surrounding his job, I had found a rewarding job as a university teacher and counselor, so I spent increasingly more time in my own studies and work. We lived together as always, but grew further apart as each went down a separate path. He had his work and relationships with his students, and I had mine. I was excited about my work and had found other people I enjoyed being with because they were good sounding boards for my own developmental process. Since few of these people were affirmed Christians, *I felt I could talk about anything with them and be accepted.* I was also studying human development and realized there was something seriously wrong with myself, our marriage, or both. I was working hard to understand my discontent and wasn't sleeping well. I would get up in the middle of the night and write. Through these memos, I began to organize my scattered thoughts into questions that needed to be answered before I could move on with my personal development and fix my marriage. Slowly, my unique purpose on earth was emerging. If we could repair our broken marriage, then we could help others with their marriages. In 1979, I wrote:

> Perhaps God's purpose for us is to teach others not only the fundamentals of living a Christian life, but the techniques of forming and maintaining a Christian marriage in a world that has changed drastically from the Christian couple that the New Testament defines, a life where the woman has taken on a completely different role in the world outside the church. Maybe my purpose in this life is to help show how it is possible for a Christian woman to fulfill God's commands for caring for her family and at the same time have an influence on people of the world through a normal, secular job that any man might also hold.
>
> Through our Christian marriage and genuine concern for each other and for our children, we can help disprove some of the traditions in the church that give women no place in this modern world. When I read the Bible through the eyes of my traditional upbringing, I can find nothing that tells me not to live a happy life just because I'm married and have children. It does not say there is only one way to be a good wife and mother. Surely, God has left the manner in which we achieve his directives up to us; otherwise, his original purpose for women was not on an equal basis with man. And God has said through Jesus, loud and clear, that all people are equal.
>
> If this is the reason I've been placed on this earth, with the rebellious, restless spirit I have, then how can I go about getting my message across to other Christians without ruining my credibility?

As usual, I formulated a type of happy ending to keep myself going, but several issues surfaced here that needed definition. Frequent mention of women's role and their lack of equality emerged. I could not comprehend a God who did not consider men and women equal. It seemed sacrilegious to question the belief system which had been instilled in me as a child, but it was vital to my own mental health and spiritual journey.

5

Questioning the Church's Teachings

DURING THE 1970S, ONE of the specific issues that clouded my already murky brain was the teaching in the church regarding a woman's role. Based on the interpretation of the Scriptures that warned women to be submissive and quiet, we were not allowed to speak in a worship service. Women in our denomination, at that time and still in most congregations today, only opened their mouths to sing. Everything else—prayers, sermons, communion thoughts, announcements—was planned and implemented by the men. It did not seem to matter how intelligent or knowledgeable the men were who led in the service; any man who wanted to could speak. I began to shut out what was going on around me during the worship service. In one of the congregations we attended, when I tried to speak in a non-worship setting such as a business meeting of the congregation, I sensed some unspoken but clear disapproval from the most visible leader and his family. This behavior may not have been planned to keep me in my "proper place," but it had that effect. The hidden message was that women were in a subordinate role to all men, not just their husbands, and not just in the worship setting. Most men considered women subordinate to them in every realm of our society. As the years and then decades passed and I continued to sit quietly, I wondered what was going on in the minds of other women, many of whom were quite intelligent and often professional women who had leadership roles in society. What were they thinking? Why did they stay? I knew why I stayed. It was for my husband and my family; otherwise, I would have looked for a church more suitable to my talents.

Another reason I stayed was that my husband was not telling me to be quiet or submissive. He occasionally mentioned that he had some of the same concerns I did. He interpreted 1 Peter 3:1–12 to mean that both men and women were to be in submission to each other. Men are to be submissive to their wives and wives submissive to their husbands, and both submissive to Christ. If a couple follows this interpretation of the submission passages, their relationship becomes more of a partnership where each one sacrifices to help the other fulfill his or her own calling. This can work beautifully, and it did for us, except for the unresolved issue regarding women's role in the church. The weekly reminders of my unequal position tainted our relationship. Just below the surface, there was a lingering concern that needed to be resolved, but we were not talking about it openly. Every attempt to discuss it ended in conflict, so we learned to avoid the topic. As we both gained experience communicating and dealing with conflict outside the home, we began to try the same techniques at home. I would try not to wait until I was frustrated to the point of anger to bring up topics that needed to be resolved. Gary acquired the technique of remaining composed when frustrated sooner than I did, but, with practice, we gradually began to communication better on touchy subjects.

When couples do not take the time to discuss the issues that are simmering below the surface, then the problem becomes magnified. To come to an agreement on what the problem truly is and some possible solutions requires open and lengthy communication. I often interpreted his words as a criticism of me, and even felt he was taking the side of others against me. As a result, I felt that I stood alone, so I tried to work through my confusion without the benefit of others' input. The question to be addressed was: Was I the problem, or was the teaching of the church leaders a wrong interpretation?

CONFRONTING THE ISSUE: THE CHURCH OR ME?

Sunday, the day of the week that is supposed to be a day of rest, has seldom been calm, peaceful, and restful for me. During my period of intense restlessness, Sunday was the worst day of the week because of the extra duties I had to assume as a result of Gary's job and the necessity that I prepare for the week ahead. Because I worked outside the home, I did not have Monday to recover from the demanding weekend. But I felt I could not be honest about how I felt; it was irreverent to hate Sundays. Gary did not want to hear any criticism of the church, so I suffered in silence except for a few memos I wrote on the subject. Portions of them were even written during church, because that was when the urge came and was often the only time I had to write. It was my therapy. It kept me from totally losing my mind.

September 5, 1982
Re: I feel like a hypocrite

Here I am again, sitting in a dull Bible class, trying not to appear too bored. I must stay awake. Last week I didn't, and it hurt the teacher's feelings. We're studying the priesthood, which doesn't strike me as very vital to my survival. Why study the priesthood? That is such a distant, vague, and unimportant subject to me. I need to study repeatedly Christian attitudes and practical living concepts. For instance, how in my life, which is totally encompassed by doing for others, do I find time or energy to read a few Scriptures a day, much less study in depth the concept of priesthood?

I don't even want to be here at all, smiling, acting interested. . . . I would much prefer to, and be spiritually uplifted much more by, staying at home, alone, listening to some well-written, well-performed Christian music. . . . Why don't we ever discuss the role of the minister's wife? Why do they assume that we're all alike, all 100 percent dedicated to a life of sacrifice and support to our husband's occupation? Personality type, individual needs, talents, and weaknesses are never considered. Every minister's wife must:

- Be a super time and money manager.

- Be interested in staying home and not working outside the home.

- Be willing to push into the subconscious any dreams of her own.

- Have little or no personal ambition.

- Have little curiosity to learn, unless it's about the Bible or Christian family life.

- Not be too attractive so that she would be a temptation to men other than her husband or a source of envy to other women; therefore, it would be well for her to be slightly chubby but definitely not overweight to the point that it is obvious she has little discipline.

- Not be outspoken and direct about the church problems she sees.

- Not be a leader. She must be willing to let others control her life, and yet at times she must assume the leadership role when no one else is willing to assume it. Therefore, she must be a master of gentle persuasion.

- Not spend too much money on her clothes, so she can't dress well unless she can let everyone know that she is one of the best bargain shoppers around. If she goes the route of not trying to dress herself or her children well, though, she will be criticized for not caring about the image of the church.

- Have an extremely clean, orderly house with furniture only slightly worn. She must make a small house large enough to hold neatly all her family's belongings and still have room for entertaining. And, of course, her children must, in spite of the crowded circumstances, not be heard while the company is there.

- Be an extremely wise shopper and cook so, that on a low budget, she can entertain well and often, though seldom will the favor be returned. Few people feel the need or have the courage to invite the minister and his family to dinner.

- Be willing to never see her husband except when others are around.

I did not share these memos with anyone. I did not dare expose my cynicism. I could not let others know how pessimistic I had become about the church, because it would hurt my husband's job and, of course, our marriage. This memo had no happy ending because I was angry. A month later, another long memo about Sundays was produced.

October 17, 1982
Re: And they call it a day of rest
It's Sunday again. I get tired just thinking of all I have to do today: Sunday school, 9:30; worship, 10:30; dinner for college students, 1:00; chorus practice for the students, 5:00; evening worship, 6:00, and Dollar Dinner and devotional for students, 7:00–9:00.

If my calculations are correct, I have three hours to accomplish everything necessary to get through the week ahead: finish the laundry, clean the house, grade papers for one of the two classes I am teaching, prepare a handout to take to printing services so it will be back by Wednesday. These are the things that absolutely must be done today. I'll try not to think about the mending, unanswered letters, baking, and the many motherly duties that have to be slighted because of the duties I have inherited from my husband's job as a minister and my job outside the home.

It's true that I would have plenty of time to accomplish all these duties plus some if I had not chosen the life of a career woman. Sundays would not be restful days, but they would be bearable if I weren't trying to accomplish most of my household duties in two days instead of five or six as do those who stay at home.

I can only fantasize about a typical Sunday then. I would still have only three hours of discretionary time, but what would I do with it? First, last night's dinner dishes would be done and the kitchen would closely resemble cleanliness. It's certainly good that the phrase "cleanliness is next to Godliness" isn't really found in the Bible as many suggest. After the dishes, if the phone or doorbell wouldn't change my plans, I would sneak into my bedroom, pull that book I've been trying to read for a month from under the stack of clothes to be folded, snuggle into my rocker and read for an hour. The last free hour of my day would be divided between the kids, listening to their chatter about the coming week.

The end result of having three leisurely hours instead of hectic ones might be disappointing because I wouldn't have the satisfaction of knowing that I had accomplished, once more, more than was humanly possible in a few hours, and feel I had sacrificed any leisure time I had to work for the Lord.

Well, that's enough of the fantasy world, and now back to reality. How can I best use my Sunday afternoon to accomplish what realistically must be done? My only strategies are to (1) set a few priorities in case everything can't be done, and (2) delegate duties to my children, so that they not only learn responsibility but learn to work cooperatively with others, and at the same time enjoy themselves.

The purpose of the solution at the end of the memo was something to keep me going, because it was not necessarily the truth. I cannot recall that any of my children ever *enjoyed* helping me clean the house. The memo did not actually end, though the color of the ink changed, so I believe now that I wrote the first half during church and then continued on after I came home, or perhaps even on another day. The entire memo was written on pages from a small, yellow pad, something I learned always to carry in my purse.

Sunday, even though extremely busy, wouldn't be so bad if I didn't feel I was being a hypocrite a good deal of the time. I honestly do not enjoy going to church very often. Sitting still is difficult for me, especially when I have so many other things calling me to be active. Church services are seldom uplifting and encouraging; they often leave me upset instead so that it is difficult to be energetic and highly motivated the rest of the day.

Sermons, for one thing, seldom center around what I feel Christians need to get through this hectic world—practical subjects, such as how to handle communication problems at home, church, and on the job. Also, how to rear our children to be strong Christians in a world of indifference to Christian values, and how to meet the needs of those around us who are so obviously lacking in many areas of their lives. I should feel guilty for my lack of love for the "brethren," since I don't always enjoy being with them, but I don't. I feel, instead, imposed upon and trapped. Because my husband's choice of profession centers around the church, it is assumed that my life should be the same. I want to cry out, "I'm an individual, I have a mind of my own; I have a personality and a set of needs separate from my husband's." Why should I be continually frustrated because I have pushed my own needs and ambitions into the background to guarantee that my husband fulfills his obligations to the church?

Over the years, I came to understand the anger that erupted from having to be overly involved in church activities. My interpretation of the anger at the time varied depending on the specific activity. At times, it was directed at the church; sometimes it was aimed at Gary, because I felt abandoned or neglected by him or obligated to become involved in activities because of his role in the church. But, most of the time, the source of the frustration was related to needing time for my own pursuits and not having time for them because of demands from church functions. Frequently, these functions were social, and social gatherings were never high on my list of priorities. I inherited from my simple roots on the farm a need to be involved in helping the underdog in society, leaving me with little time for socializing. In spite of this, to improve our marriage, I felt I must participate to support Gary. So, I became actively involved in some functions and chose not to attend others. I enjoyed music, so I helped form and lead a chorus for students. We had small groups of students to our house on weekends so that I could remain with the family and still fulfill my obligations as a minister's wife. Gary also compromised. He took our children on special outdoor activities with the students, leaving me free to pursue activities I enjoyed or to get the household chores completed.

A minister's job security depends to a great extent on church members' impressions of him and his family. He is judged not only by what he says or does, but also by his family's behavior. A natural outcome of this continual judgment is, I believe, a type of paranoia, where individuals begin to think they are being watched and judged by people in the church. This is based on reality, the fact that many ministers and their families live in a glass house where they are expected to be perfect at all times. If not, they are criticized. And most people within the congregation feel it is their right to tell the minister and his wife how to live their lives. In our case, there was some foundation for this paranoia, but it was distorted because I can identify very few people who were openly judging us. In fact, many of our Christian friends over those years of struggling with work and family were quite supportive. One woman kept our daughter for three weeks when she had chicken pox and had to stay out of preschool. But paranoia is not based on facts; it is a distortion of reality. I generalized my feelings about a few people who made remarks about my husband's and children's behavior to the church in general.

In one of my memos about the church, the topic changed slightly to discuss working women. As far as I was concerned, this was a related topic because of the teachings of some church leaders and ministers (and their wives) that kept women in a secondary role. Teachings regarding women's role in the church had been broadened to keep women in a subordinate place in society, at home "where they belong."[1] That was extremely frustrating to me because the argument simply was not logical.

> If women don't work, then men, in these hard times, have to hold down an extra job to make ends meet, which means that their wives are left alone satisfying their husband's and children's needs and withdrawing more and more into their shells, causing emotional, mental, and physical illnesses beyond repair. Unsatisfied needs will inevitably cause these illnesses.
>
> The majority of women today are encouraged to go to college, open their minds to worlds of information, become logical and careful thinkers, competing in the classroom, only to be told, upon marriage to a Christian, who is supposed to be understanding and open to others' needs, that you must follow the New Testament teachings and stay at home, being in subjection to your husbands and caring for the needs of their families.
>
> This narrow interpretation of the Scriptures and totally ignorant approach to understanding individual needs must be combated. Women must declare their needs to their husbands and to the church leaders, and educate them about the real needs of educated women in the church.

I was angry and rebellious, but again afraid to tell anyone how I felt. I was living in a region of the country where church leaders and, as far as I knew, most of the women I encountered were not open-minded about changing roles in society. If a woman with children worked outside the

1. The source of this feeling is a little foggy today, but I remember thinking when attending a Christian college lectureship that no one was writing books about the life I was attempting to live. They were all about women who did not work outside the home.

home, it was considered wrong. I never actually heard anyone say I was sinning, but I felt it whenever I was around certain individuals, mainly women, and was treated by some as if I had a contagious disease. I suppose, in their minds, I was considered a liberal person who had fallen into the hands of the feminists. Actually, I knew nothing about feminists at this point in my life, but many Christian writers (men and women) in our country evidently thought they did, because the word *feminist*, or more often *women's libber*, was used to label any woman who went against the traditional role for women.[2]

A TEMPORARY RESOLUTION

It is difficult, usually impossible, when you are in the midst of crises or even daily hassles to see clearly what the source of the problem is, so some of us blame our spouses, and others blame the church and leave it behind. And, I'm afraid, too frequently because of their insecurities, women take full responsibility for the problems. I can now, after many years of studying, say that the source of my own marriage issues was a combination of many factors, not the fault of either of us. First, there were unrealistic social expectations for mothers and wives in general in society, and especially for Christian wives. Second, there was a contradiction between my upbringing and the world I had landed in, having been raised without much exposure to the wider society, so I made a decision about getting married at a very young age without understanding what was ahead. Third, I had some unresolved developmental issues from earlier stages of life. These did not go away without serious introspection. And last, my husband and I were mismatched in some very important areas, but in particular, our life goals were not the same. We both had admirable goals that included dedicated service to others, but the manner in which we wanted to serve and the population we were interested in serving were quite different.

Two divergent sets of goals could not be met within our marriage; one of us had to sacrifice his or her goals, or we both had to compromise, which is what we eventually did. In spite of the many problems, we both

---

2. Some of the books I ran across in the 1970s included Boggs, *Is a Job Really Worth It?*, which advocates that a Christian woman must stay home with her children until they are grown and presents many negative interpretations on why women work outside the home. See also Green, *What Are We Doing Here?* and Morgan, *The Total Woman*.

were committed to making our marriage work, so I continually sought solutions for at least twenty years. The word "I" is quite revealing here. My husband did not feel the need for our marriage to change; he was quite satisfied with our marriage and thought I was also. He was not, at the time, aware of the content of the "memos to myself."

One area where we compromised was actually initiated by one of our sons. Mark, our middle child, asked if we could have fewer people in our home. So we lessened the social aspect of entertaining other Christians and I concentrated on building relationships within our family, seeking ways to involve Gary with the children. He kept the children one night a week while I went to school; therefore, I could pursue my long-term need to learn more about human behavior. Gary and I also scheduled time to get away from the church and demands of our jobs and engage in something fun, an aspect of our relationship that had been neglected for years. We went to concerts, movies, and long weekends in retreat from the pressures of the world.

When we could not escape the stresses of our lives, a temporary solution that always worked for me, though I could not label it, was one of *delayed gratification*. I continually postponed the fulfilling of my own needs. I later learned from M. Scott Peck's writings that this is a healthy mechanism for handling problems that are out of our control.[3] Delayed gratification was a strategy that kept me from doing something radical that I would regret later, like leaving my husband and children.

From a lifespan development perspective, I was stuck in the middle of adolescence, but my marriage and family situation prevented me from completing the psychological work necessary to move on to the next stage in life. My internal alarm clock was ringing. I felt a sense of urgency to finish the developmental work that I had started in my teens. I needed what Erikson referred to as a *moratorium*, time away from the demands of daily living.[4] I was working full time, keeping house, cooking, providing support to my husband, and attending the same church I had attended as a child, thereby following in my parents' footsteps without making a conscious decision to do so. I fought the urge to run away to Mexico (we lived in the Southwest). I think I wanted to escape

---

3. Peck's *The Road Less Traveled*, published in 1978, was on the bestseller list for many years. Once I was introduced to it, I read it repeatedly because it helped me deal with the upsets in my own life.

4. Erikson, *Identity, Youth, and Crisis*.

to a place where no one knew me. I had never been allowed to explore my world and discover who I was as a unique person. In spite of that, I became a responsible adult, but it was an *imitation of life*—simply a role I played. I felt like I was an actress on a stage, not a real person. I was doing what I was expected to do.

Delayed gratification kept me from completely giving up on my own dream to do something special with my life, though I still did not know what that "something" would be. The question became: How can I fulfill this dream? A long memo written in October 1982, at age 38, concluded with a solution:

> The answer to this may be: be patient about "setting the world on fire." Take care of first things first. My top priority now must be for a few more years to be primarily supportive to my husband and children—get them through their critical periods, but never allow myself to quit thinking about my ultimate goal.
>
> I must keep recording my thoughts as I have been on Christian marriage, working women, and childrearing, and keep reevaluating not only my situation, but also those of many women who are fighting the same battles I am.
>
> I must prepare myself in such a way that people will listen when I do eventually find a means of transmitting my ideas. What do I need to make me more convincing?
>
> I must learn to enjoy studying the Bible, and, with a set goal, it will be easier.
>
> I must somehow expose myself to all different types of family problems—not just the working women issue, but also the plight of the woman who chooses not to work in a world where most women do.
>
> I must learn about the problems of the family that don't have all the normal advantages that we have:
> - the single/divorced Christian
> - the Christian family with little education and money
> - the needs of the elderly Christian family
>
> I have so much to learn that it will take me just about as many years of my life as my children need, so the two main goals of my life must be (1) raising my children and (2) beginning the task of converting traditional beliefs about the Christian woman and family into a more workable, modern situation.

Once again, I had a positive ending. I had set a goal to work on, something that was manageable because it was related to the duties that were necessary to keep my marriage and family afloat, but also something that could lead to the fulfilling of my personal goal of doing something meaningful with my life. The problem with this happy-ending habit of mine was that it was not founded on my authentic self. It was a creation of the person I was trying to become, because that was what others expected of me and what I thought had to happen to keep my marriage and family intact. This technique, though, kept me in the marriage and bought us the time necessary to understand the problem and arrive at long-term solutions, such as learning and using better communication skills. We also began to educate ourselves on our different styles of communicating and tried to understand each other's needs better. I learned how total involvement with the church was absolutely vital to Gary's life, and he began to understand how necessary it was for me to pursue further education and work at jobs that I felt were meaningful. My involvement in these activities prevented me from being as involved in church work as he was, but he accepted that. Probably the most important change we made, though it was a gradual process, was to allow each other time to talk about his or her daily activities and what we were thinking about our worlds in general. In time, we could discuss without tension our differences in religious philosophy and church practices.

6

Reflecting Back over Life

> There is a yearning deep within me that is never satisfied and is perhaps indefinable, but I think the yearning is to return to the childhood of peace that I once knew, a childhood that demanded very little of me.[1]

IN 1994, AT AGE fifty, I completed my PhD in human development and had absorbed every book and article I could find on female psychological development. By this time, articles and books on women's psychology were abundant and helped me design a theoretical identity development process based on the experiences of more than forty women I interviewed for my dissertation. My research also helped me complete the puzzle of my own development. With much more knowledge of society and women's psychology, answers were finally appearing for questions I had earlier. Reflecting on my life in the 1990s was much more productive than doing so in the 1970s.

As I reflected back over my life, reading *The Girl Within* by Emily Hancock clarified why I had experienced so much turmoil in giving up my childhood dream of becoming a teacher in India. Hancock had, like me, spent a number of years of her life studying women's development, identifying what she called the *inner girl*, the little girl always with us, even into adulthood.

> At the buried core of women's identity is a distinct and vital self first articulated in childhood, a root identity that gets cut off in the process of growing up female. [Women] come fully into their own and become truly themselves only when they recapture the girl they'd been in the first place—before she got all cluttered up.[2]

1. Memo to myself, November 1982.
2. Hancock, *The Girl Within*, 3.

Hancock explains how our early childhood dreams are pushed to the subconscious as little girls enter adolescence and comply with society's expectations. They gradually lose sight of their authentic self as they form the mask that helps them survive in society. Who is this inner girl? It is the girl of our past who is content with herself:

> . . . one who pulls on her blue jeans, packs her own lunch, and gets on her bike to ride to her best friend's house to build a fort or a tree house. Liberated from the confines of the family, she is proud of her newfound ability to order and direct her life. It is at this age that a girl gets her first wristwatch, sets her own alarm clock, and chooses her own clothes. A superb organizer, she is likely to have her own collection of stamps, stones, shells, or snake skins—or perhaps bugs or birds' nests.
>
> Often a tomboy, she may be a gymnast or a sleuth—or a junior scientist whose prize possession is her own microscope. No matter what her particular bent, this independent and adventurous girl has many capabilities. Her competence at home and school grows in one long, upward sweep. Heady with the power that comes from genuine competence, she brims with initiative.[3]

When I read Hancock's words, my mind flashed back to my childhood on the farm in Colorado where I grew up. It was the 1950s, a time historians describe as idyllic. The survivors of World War II, later labeled the "greatest generation," were happy to be alive and wanted a simple life of working and raising a family. My life was also simple. Like Hancock's girl, I collected things; in my case, it was insects—black-widow spiders. I held one of my mother's canning jars close to the ground and watched the spider enter my trap. Then I transferred the spider into a small bottle filled with rubbing alcohol, replaced the cap, and placed him in the cellar with my other victims, next to my mother's jars of canned vegetables. I had waged my own war—ridding the world of evil, in the form of black-widow spiders.

The farm where we lived was truly peaceful. There was no television broadcasting the bad news in the world. Talk of the Cold War and McCarthy's communists was unheard of, at least by me. The only things I had to fear were more concrete: coyotes, rattlesnakes, and black-widow spiders. I had taken care of the spiders and learned how to deal with rattlesnakes. It seemed to be common knowledge, when one spied a

---

3. Ibid., 9.

rattlesnake, she should freeze and watch the snake carefully avoid the obstacle, not knowing what it was. So I spent hours by myself exploring the outdoor world of the Colorado Desert and farmlands. Hancock describes this free spirit as independence and one with a "soaring imagination":

> A girl this age can aspire to far-reaching objectives in her imagination—a new and private inner realm no one else is privy to. There, if nowhere else, her ambitions are boundless; anything is possible.[4]

My inner thoughts flourished during the hours I spent walking alone across my parents' farm. Large sand dunes looked to me like Native American teepees,[5] so they became the homes of my imaginary friends. We "talked" about whatever *I* wanted to discuss. I didn't have to yield to adults, who typically thought that children were to be seen and not heard. When I was on my walks around the farm, no one bothered me. I could live uninterrupted and safely in my make-believe world. Since my parents talked very little to each other or to my brother and me, they never asked about my adventures.

I grew too old to daydream, but continued it anyway, wondering sometimes what was wrong with me. It was the only way I could process my thoughts because, in those days, teenagers were not allowed to use the phone to talk to friends and, of course, there were no emails or text messages. Also, I had not yet started writing. Basically, my childhood world was uneventful and, as Hancock described, pleasant.

> For this short period, the culture permits her respite from its construction of the female. . . . Liberated from feminine constraints, her world encompasses male and female, work and play, independence and dependence—without subordinating either to the other. At the center of a universe in perfect harmony, in step with family, friends and schoolmates, she is master of her destiny, captain of her soul. She is, in short, the subject of her own experience.[6]

But, unknown to me, my world changed, or I changed so that I had to grow up and act like a little lady.

---

4. Ibid.

5. My only exposure to Native Americans was through books, so I assumed they still lived in teepees.

6. Hancock, *The Girl Within*, 9–10.

WHAT BECOMES OF THE GIRL WITHIN?

Like my world of imaginary playmates, which practically disappeared overnight, the same thing happens to young girls everywhere:

> Suddenly, well before puberty, along comes the culture with the pruning shears, ruthlessly trimming back her spirit. Adults who left the girl to her own devices anticipate her blossoming femininity and nip her expansion in the bud. As the culture draws the line between little and big, play and work, female and male, its agents feel, despite themselves, obliged to intervene. Old templates of female as nurturer persist, making a girl's boundless initiative threatening.
>
> Seldom permitted to be a tomboy once her features begin to change, she is expected, even now, to "behave like a young lady."[7]

One day, I was playing with insects and exploring the outdoors, and the next thing I knew, I was wearing red, three-inch high heels to a high school banquet and hating every minute of it. I have a picture of myself in this transition. I wore the perfect dress and shoes to make me look like a girl, but my hair was still the tomboyish style I preferred.

> While her brother is encouraged to flex his muscles and test his mettle, she is turned to feminine compliance.
>
> She is returned to her mother—returned to the women's world, she is drawn into the cave of womanly doings.
>
> Her mother may subtly shape her activities to fit feminine stereotypes, training her daughter in the same roles that have defined her as wife and mother.
>
> Impressed with the importance of others' opinions, she molds herself to what she thinks they want her to be.[8]

Many years later, from Hancock's book and the more academic writings of Carol Gilligan,[9] I gradually pieced together a framework of how little girls develop into adult women and had an idea of what became of my perfect world of childhood. My training to become a woman was so subtle and swift that, practically overnight, a small, lively child with dreams of changing the world transformed into the woman that my

7. Ibid., 18.
8. Ibid., 18–19.
9. Gilligan, *In a Different Voice.*

family, friends, and society in general *wanted me to be.* And, in my case, without being consciously aware of it, I became what a "good Christian girl" should be. If Brown and Gilligan[10] had included me in their study of young adolescent girls, they would not have been surprised. They discovered that the female development progress is like a two-edged sword. As they grow older, girls become less dependent on external authorities for their self-definition and quite able to take responsibilities for themselves, but, at the same time, they show evidence of a loss of voice:

> [W]e found that this developmental progress goes hand in hand with evidence of a loss of voice, a struggle to authorize or take seriously their own experience—to listen to their own voices in conversation and respond to their feelings and thoughts—increased confusion, sometimes defensiveness, as well as evidence for the replacement of real with inauthentic or idealized relationships. . . . These girls are in fact not developing, but are showing evidence of loss and struggle and signs of an impasse in their ability to act in the face of conflict.[11]

Brown and Gilligan consider the girls they studied to be in the midst of a developmental crisis: "[T]he crossroads between girls and women is marked by a series of disconnections or dissociations which leave girls psychologically at risk and involved in a relational struggle,"[12] a struggle that often remains throughout early adulthood.

Although it is not in their conscious awareness, little girls are subtly taught from birth how they are supposed to "be" in the world. They are surrounded by pink, frilly, feminine clothes. They watch movies and read stories about pretty girls who are delicate and gracious—perfect in every way. Stories of love and romance are presented by Disney in the forms of *The Little Mermaid, Beauty and the Beast, Cinderella, Snow White,* and numerous other stories with a princess as the heroine. My little granddaughter, Sydney, who entered this world with a strong will and, by age two, had the physical strength to tackle her older brother, became, by age three, totally engrossed in the idea of "Sydney, the princess." She loved the princess movies, wanted to look like a princess by wearing dresses all the time, even in the dead of winter, and knew by heart the theme songs from most of the Disney princess movies. When she sang the love songs, she even took on the dreamy look shown in the

10. Brown and Gilligan, *Meeting at the Crossroads.*
11. Ibid., 6.
12. Ibid.

movies. Her favorite pretend play included Ariel kissing Eric (from *The Little Mermaid*). Wrestling with her brother and playing outdoors took a back seat to princess themes.

Why does one girl choose to be like a little princess and another decide to become a basketball star? It essentially comes down to what parents emphasize or allow into their girls' lives. If a little girl is exposed to sports and is encouraged to be athletic and praised for her athletic ability, she will, most likely, become interested in and good at sports. If a little girl is submerged in feminine themes in movies, books, and in her daily life and praised for how pretty or feminine she looks, she will place her emphasis there. She will imitate this aspect of other girls and women and build permanent neural connections in the brain that present, in her mind, a little girl as feminine. As this girl matures, she will discover that a large part of being feminine in our society entails taking care of others—soothing hurt feelings, cooking for and waiting on others, and being good and polite. In other words, she will soon realize that she needs to be perfect, and she will do everything in her power to become the person she has fashioned in her mind. Gilligan and Brown describe how Jessie, an eleven-year-old girl, learned to strive for perfection:

> In a world of cliques and in-groups, the image of the perfect girl is powerful—being her can assure Jessie of inclusion, love, attention. . . . Voice training by adults, especially adult "good women," undermines these girls' experiences and reinforces images of female perfection by implying that "nice girls" are always calm, controlled, quiet, that they never cause a ruckus, are never noisy, bossy, or aggressive, are not anxious and do not cause trouble, and also by implying that such girls exist and are desirable.[13]

And so, experience after experience reinforces a little girl's image of how she is supposed to act in her world. What happens, then, to this little girl as she grows into an adult?

TRANSITION TO ADULTHOOD

As she nears puberty, an unsuspecting child is suddenly asked to grow up. When the hormones take over, parents seem to panic and assume their little girls are totally different people. They initiate for their daughters a new set of rules different from those they give their sons. For the girls, pressure to conform is tremendous: *What can I do to make myself*

13. Ibid., 61.

pretty and feminine? becomes the most pressing issue. Because the pressure is embedded in our society, few adolescent girls escape it, even if their parents are more flexible and understanding.

In my case, it was after I entered high school that my life began to change so drastically. I no longer played baseball and quit listening to the Yankees and Dodgers games on the radio. As a freshman in high school, I played on a girls' basketball team during gym class, but since girls were not allowed to compete in the state of Colorado—it was not considered safe for them—I gradually lost interest in sports. I think of that policy frequently these days because, in the twenty-first century, women's basketball has become a popular spectator sport. In many ways, the world has changed for girls, but there are still those who want to marry a prince. In the 1950s, to become another Cinderella was still the goal of most adolescent girls, though it was not something we necessarily verbalized. We, especially white, middle-class girls, just *knew* what we were supposed to do was find a Prince Charming to take care of us.[14]

CINDERELLA, DRESSED IN YELLOW

When I entered the ninth grade in 1958, I not only quit sports, but also added home economics courses to my curriculum and joined Future Homemakers of America, an organization for young women planning on a career in homemaking. I am not sure at what age I began to go to my local library and check out books to read, but I remember during my adolescent years reading an entire book nearly every day during the summer months. Unfortunately, I had no guidance about what I should be reading, so I checked out teenage romance novels. Among these was a series of books written by Grace Livingston Hill about young Christian women who were extremely good girls and consequently were rewarded by having handsome, yet wholesome, young men fall in love with them. It was the two of them against the world and they always won the battle. Then, they got married and lived happily ever after. A Christian version of the Cinderella story filled my mind with visions of what my future would be. This simplistic and naive interpretation of womanhood was later to become the source of much uncertainty, frustration, and rebellion.

14. When I began to interview women in the 1990s, one of the most noticeable differences between Caucasian and African American women was that African American women were taught they had to take care of themselves. Their mothers told them there would be no Prince Charming to provide for them.

It seems impossible now that I was so immature that I did not realize what really lay ahead for me. My mother's life was extremely difficult; she appeared never to have fun, and her relationship with my dad, though not bad, was nothing like Cinderella and the Prince. Most of the girls I went to high school with had no real plans for after graduation except getting married and settling down right there in Colorado. I do not even remember discussing the topic with my friends. It seemed to be an implicit belief that we were to be wives and mothers when we were grown. But I felt I was different. I suppose I felt that, if I got away from that farming community, I would meet an ideal young man and my life would be different.

By the time I left for college, I had a somewhat cloudy vision of what I wanted my life to be for the next ten years. Dating, going steady, and getting engaged were not anything I seriously thought about, though I did like the notion of falling in love and sharing my dreams with someone. The songs I heard on the radio—*Love Me Tender* by Elvis Presley and *Dream, Dream, Dream* by the Everly Brothers—filled my mind with ideas of romance. I also saw a few movies that reinforced the fairy tale that women would fall in love, get married, and live happily ever after. The movie *Giant* presented a young beautiful girl falling in love with a handsome dreamboat. Fifty years later, I can still clearly see this young girl riding in a convertible with her hair flying in the wind and her male admirer being totally captivated by her. The same theme was present in *Oklahoma*, one of the first movies I ever saw and ultimately the first soundtrack my brother and I owned. All of these cultural offerings reinforced the feminine ideal that was shaping the way I perceived my place in the world.

7

Acquiring Masks

RUTH BENEDICT, AN ANTHROPOLOGIST who lived from 1887 to 1948, four years after I was born, wrote about how women acquire masks as they attempt to find their place in society. She presented two scenarios for women of her generation: life with marriage and children, and life without them. Benedict was twenty-five years old and unmarried when she wrote these words, showing how very complex a woman's life was in the early twentieth century:

> My real me was a creature I dared not look upon—it was ter-
> rorized by loneliness, frozen by a sense of futility obsessed by a
> longing to stop. No one had ever heard of that Me. If they had,
> they would have thought it an interesting pose. The mask was
> tightly adjusted.[1]

Benedict's language is fascinating because it describes the way I often felt. She used the same phrase I did: the real me was trying to surface, but the mask imposed upon her by the society in which she lived was winning.[2] By age twenty-five, Benedict knew that her options were quite limited because she was a woman.

> So much of the trouble is because I am a woman. To me it seems
> a very terrible thing to be a woman. There is one crown which is
> perhaps worth it all—a great love, a quiet home, and children.

---

1. Benedict, *Revelations*, 150.

2. Though it is not known whether Benedict was aware of it, psychologist Carl Jung, her contemporary, was writing about the persona, the part of an individual's psyche that directs a person's interaction with the environment. It is a healthy adaptation mechanism, but can become harmful if it "stiffens, becomes automatic, and, in the real meaning of the word, a grown-on mask behind which the individual shrivels and runs the risk of becoming ever more empty." Jacobi, *The Psychology of Jung*, 19.

We all know that is all that is worth while, and yet we must peg away, showing off our wares on the market if we have money, or manufacturing careers for ourselves if we haven't. We have not the motive to prepare ourselves for a "life-work" of teaching, of social work—we know that we would lay it down with hallelujah in the height of our success to make a home for the right man.

Then there are the girls I know in Pasadena. They are most of them ten years older than I. They are no longer young; they will probably never marry. They are fighting the ennui of a life without a purpose. Some of them are studying shorthand, some are taking music lessons, one just embroiders. They are doing their best—to trump up a reason for living. And within a year they'll find that there is no virtue even in a pay envelope to make life seem worth living.

The trouble is not that we are never happy—it is that happiness is so episodical. A morning in the library, an afternoon with someone I really care about, a day in the mountains, a good-night-time with the babies [her sister's children] can almost frighten me with happiness. But then, it is gone and I cannot see what holds it all together. What is worth while? What is the purpose? What do I *want*?[3]

Ruth Benedict later married, but, by 1934, was separated from her husband and working as an anthropologist. Somewhere along the way, she had acquired a PhD in anthropology. She had tried both the traditional role for women, as a wife, and a life as a professional woman, but was not happy with either. Perhaps she would have been happy as a professional woman with a family as so many women are now, but that was not an option in the early 1900s.

The writings of other women who lived in the same era as Ruth Benedict and in earlier times began to appear in the 1980s and 1990s in the form of graduate theses and then biographies and collections of letters. Gradually, as I immersed myself in these writings, I discovered themes that had been present for at least two hundred years among women who were not content to follow society's prescription for them. They chose to be independent and unique. As they went from childhood to adulthood, they made conscious decisions to act on the difference they had always felt—to do with their lives what their hearts dictated. Unlike Ruth Benedict, they chose to become their real selves, not wear-

3. Benedict, in Moffatt and Painter, *Revelations*, 153.

ing masks. Most of these women, however, remained unmarried because they felt they could not be unique and also fulfill the duties of a wife and mother.

In the late twentieth century, women were determined to do it all—to be successful career women as well as wives and mothers. Many remained confused, depressed, or angry and ended up in therapy so they could manage their multiple lives. Dana Crowley Jack, a psychotherapist whose clients included these women attempting to fill both roles, became dissatisfied with traditional explanations for women's mental health issues and completed in-depth research with women in an attempt to understand their lack of aggression.[4] Jack describes our society as one that creates in young girls a fear of being unfeminine and consequently disliked by their friends, and especially boys. As these girls grow into adulthood, they become even more confused. Although they are told they can do anything with their lives, including competing with men in the workplace, competing successfully in many careers requires a certain amount of aggression. Jack refers to a "puzzle of aggression" where women attempt to distinguish between positive aggression, which is needed in the workplace and to maintain equality in intimate relationships, and the more negative aggression that results in a woman being labeled as too pushy. Women's attempt to determine the correct femininity often results in depression and anger.

In my case, the real me was an independent, strong-willed person who craved the freedom to explore the world. But instead, after I married my prince, I wore a mask that portrayed me as a compliant, subordinate wife. Without the help of a therapist or knowledge of women's psychology, I did not understand that the mask I wore was created by the social norm of a woman's place being in the home. I was unaware of the stories of Ruth Benedict and other women like her who struggled with their identities. But the memos I wrote from 1976 to 1984 had one underlying core theme: I was struggling to find my real self and to become an authentic person. I was attempting to peel away the masks I had acquired from my childhood, adolescence, and young adulthood.

---

4. Jack has written two books on women's psychological development: *Silencing the Self*, which describes women's loss of self, self-condemnation, and hopelessness, and *Behind the Mask*, which addresses the difficulty women face as they attempt to fulfill societal expectations to be compliant, nurturing individuals and yet successful in careers that sometimes require aggression.

During the 1950s when my masks were being created, women were back in the home, many feeling rather content because they had survived difficult times during World War II. The economy was good, there were many gadgets to buy for the home, and the men who had served overseas deserved to be pampered. Though I do not remember my mother ever pampering anyone, my dad was a veteran, and the security of knowing that he was home with his family must have contributed to our relatively happy home life. My mother had been schooled in the basics of being a good wife by her mother and probably her older sisters. Farm men worked extremely hard six days of the week, usually taking Sunday off to attend church and socialize with friends and neighbors. Because they worked so hard, they deserved special treatment when they arrived home.

Some of the literature of the times contributed to the "good wife" persona for which young girls of the times were being groomed. For example, a 1955 magazine article offered advice on how a good wife was supposed to behave: "Have a delicious meal ready on time for his return. This is a way of letting him know that you have been thinking about him and are concerned about his needs."[5] My mother followed this advice to the T. She cooked delicious meals, but I doubt it entered her mind to do it so my dad would know she was thinking about him. She was simply following the routine that farm women had always followed. To work hard day after day requires hearty and nutritious food.

> Listen to him. You may have a dozen important things to tell him, but the moment of his arrival is not the time. Let him talk first—remember, his topics of conversation are more important than yours.[6]

There is no doubt my mother felt what men had to say was more important because she told me so many times. However, I believe that my mother seldom had important things to share with my father. She had little to say about any topic and always seemed too tired or depressed to talk at all. There were several similar rules for women to follow to be a good wife of the 1950s:

> [L]ight a fire for him to unwind by. Your husband will feel he has reached a haven or rest and order, and it will give you a lift too.

5. "Good Wife's Guide."
6. Ibid.

After all, catering for his comfort will provide you with immense personal satisfaction.

Try to make sure your home is a place of peace, order and tranquility where your husband can renew himself in body and spirit.

A good wife always knows her place.

Although many of these edicts did not apply to my mother and our life on the farm, the last one surely did. Through their religious teachings and messages from popular literature, women definitely knew their place in the home, and that is how we proper girls of the times began our education on how to be good wives. We acquired the good-little-girl masks at an early age, but were not even aware we wore them.

8

Becoming a Good Wife

IN 1970, A FEW years before I began questioning my place as a Christian woman, Helen Andelin published the first of two books that reinforced a submissive role for Christian women in society, a position that led women to acquire masks.[1] Andelin attempted to persuade girls that they should acquire the traits that made them appear wholesome as they approached the "marriageable age." She said she was trying to "offset some of the false and immoral teachings of our day,"[2] an obvious reference to feminism. A quote from Victor Hugo was displayed prominently inside the front cover:

> There is in this world no function more important than that of being charming—to spread joy around—to cast light upon dark days. Is not this to render a service?

In 1971, she published a similar book for women.[3] Some of the key concepts in this book reinforce the Cinderella and Snow White stories that so many young girls grow up hearing and absorbing into their psyches. She speaks of romantic love as "celestial love," and defines it as the "highest kind of tender love a man can feel for a woman." She considers it the "center of our happiness" and "what every woman has wanted since the world began."[4]

But, the catch is, girls must learn how to attract men who can offer this celestial love. They must, first of all, learn how to understand a man and then develop these *fascinating* qualities that men like:

1. *The Fascinating Girl.* Andelin admitted that her book was inspired by a series of booklets published in the 1920s entitled *The Secrets of Fascinating Womanhood.*

2. Andelin, *The Fascinating Girl*, preface.

3. *A Fascinating Womanhood.*

4. Andelin, *A Fascinating Womanhood*, 15.

72

Men just naturally seek the company of girls who are happy, as we all do. This inner beauty not only captivates the man's interest, but gives his spirits a lift, too, since happiness tends to be "catching." . . . Inner happiness is a quality of serenity, peace of mind, and tranquility.

Girls must be able to "cook, sew, manage a household, care for children, handle money wisely and a myriad of other things that go to make up the homemaker." And, they must have "radiant health":

The foundation of fresh beauty is genuine good health, not only for the health itself, but for the fresh and joyous spirit health sustains in the woman's appearance, actions, and attitudes. How alluring are sparkling and dancing eyes, lustrous hair, clear voice, buoyancy of manner and the animation which good health brings to the face and the vivacity it communicates to the thoughts.[5]

Other terms Andelin used that could easily be the foundation for masks are *feminine dependency*, *worthy character*, and *childlikeness*. About the same time as Andelin published her books, the popular media and academic journals began to draw attention to the fear of independence expressed by women. According to these authors, women had been programmed to be taken care of and did not know what to do when circumstances called for independence. Colette Dowling discussed some of the struggles in which women were engaged in the 1970s.[6] She cited several popular women's magazine articles that exposed the problems of working mothers. Some women appeared to be angry because the women's movement had resulted in more divorces, which in turn put them in a position where they might have to work. Dowling, who reviewed extensively journal articles written by psychotherapists and psychologists, felt that women were psychologically dependent and had deep inner conflict over whether to remain dependent or take the plunge and take care of themselves.

Women were in a no-win situation. If they stayed at home and let men take care of them, they would wonder later what they had missed. Further, if their husbands grew tired of them and got a divorce, or if their husbands died, they would be unable to support themselves. Dowling was writing about women who were born in the 1940s—my generation. Without realizing it, I had also been programmed to be taken care of.

5. Andelin, *The Fascinating Girl*, 175.
6. Dowling, *The Cinderella Complex*.

I remember a few times being angry because my husband could not take care of me. This attitude emerged when I was working in a job I did not like, wanted to take time off and go to school, or was exhausted from juggling both work and family. As my mother would have put it, I wanted my cake and to eat it too, a phrase that made little sense to me as a child. I was trying to have the best of both worlds.

Many of the women who juggled career and family became supermoms. They were brought up as nurturers and family caretakers, and they could not, without guilt, leave that role behind. So, they were determined to do it all. They would be good mothers, good wives, and good workers! Once I worked through my indecision about whether or not to work outside the home, I fell into the supermom mode. It was not a conscious move; it was simply necessary to be super-efficient and organized if I wanted to work outside the home and keep my family going. I would have to do it all because there was no one else to do it. Gary helped, but he was also trying to manage an unreasonable workload and be a husband and father.

From my work outside the home, I learned how to be efficient and organized. Although I wanted a more intellectually demanding job, an eight-to-five position is all I could manage with a young, growing family. Being in a set routine and taking no work home with me was extremely important. A fringe benefit was the opportunity to learn how to manage myself and others—time management, stress management, designing efficient workflow processes, and negotiating were all skills I learned on the job that helped me manage my relationships and functions at home. And more important, my self-esteem increased as I learned how to handle my job functions. In other words, success on the job contributed to an overall feeling of wellbeing that I could not get from being "just a mom."

In spite of these positive elements, like other women in society at the time, I felt a great deal of internal conflict, though I could not yet pinpoint the cause. So, in the 1970s, encumbered by "good little girl" masks, I was not really free to become my own person. My identity was so closely tied with my husband's that I could not create one of my own. I was a creation of society and, in particular, the Christian subculture in which I was absorbed. I had a group identity, but no personal identity, no uniqueness, no individualism. I later found the label for the state I was in: diffused identity,[7] which is normal for adolescence, but a psy-

7. See Erikson, *Identity and the Life Cycle*, and J. E. Marcia, "Identity in Adolescence"

chologically unhealthy place in adulthood. I had traveled through three major developmental stages of life—childhood, adolescence, and young adulthood—without truly growing up. I looked and acted like an adult, but I often felt like a confused, angry child.

During that same time, author Lillian Rubin was exploring the topic because of her own emotional instability. Her book expressed the same thoughts and feelings I was having.

> I am a mid-life woman. Like most women of my generation, I gave over much of my adult life to marriage and motherhood. Like so many others, I awoke one day from the childhood dream that I would be forever cared for—that being some man's wife and some child's mother would occupy my mind and my hands for the rest of my life. And I lay on my couch, listened to music, and wept with despair.
>
> I felt isolated, lonely, and furious with myself. I had a man I loved and a child I loved. What was the matter with me? Why wasn't I happy? What did I expect of life anyway?[8]

These were the same sentiments I heard from Wilma, the African American woman struggling with her role as wife and mother. As her marriage began to break down, she realized she had to finish her education so she could support herself and her son.

> So I knew that I needed school, anyway, just for my own mind and also because I could already picture that I wasn't going to be able to handle this and that I would be taking care of myself. And that's why I say the old tapes come back, and "Honey, you can't do it without some kind of education." So, then things got really bad, when I started going to school, they started snowballing for me. My tolerance level to continue with a relationship that wasn't working; I couldn't any longer deny that I just wasn't the type to be the wife, the wife-type. The things that I wanted were always in conflict with what was expected of me, that everybody else's needs came first, that mine never counted for stuff. I'm not talking about things, I'm talking about self-actualization.
>
> I didn't have the energy to put up with trying to explain things to folks, and it was heartbreaking to my grandparents when I said, "This is it. I quit." I wanted a divorce, and the first thing they asked me was, "Is he hurting you, is he abusing you, is he drinking? He's giving you this lovely home, you have worked together."

---

in Adelson, *Handbook of Adolescent Psychology.*

8. Rubin, *Women of a Certain Age,* 2.

> And I said, "I'm not happy, don't you get it? I'm not happy." And I couldn't even explain to them why I wasn't happy because it didn't make any sense to them. Once I left the marriage, it was like somebody had taken a ton weight off my mind. Not that I didn't love my husband, I care about him a great deal, even today, as a person.

Like Wilma's grandparents, I knew I had a good situation and did not have the right to complain. In comparison with women all around the world who were destitute, emotionally and physically abused, or mentally unstable, how did I have the audacity to question the life I was given? I was complaining about life not being meaningful enough, feeling it was a life-and-death matter. I was not comparing myself to those less fortunate than I, but was simply trying to find my own *unique* self. The key question revolved around my purpose in life, and finally, in the 1980s, when I discovered Carl Jung's theory regarding midlife transition, I was relieved to find that someone felt the process I had been through was psychologically healthy.

In Jungian psychology, one of the primary processes in an adult's life is that of individuation, where "a man becomes the definite, unique being he in fact is."[9] This process of individuation brings about an interpretation of the unconscious self into the mind of the conscious individual. The goal of individuation is "knowing oneself as completely as possible, or self consciousness."[10] Individuation is not the same as individualism or self-centeredness. Instead, it helps an individual fulfill his or her own specific nature and become a whole person. In Christ's words, we receive fullness (Col 2:10).

Even though I never subjected myself to psychotherapy, through twenty years of reading, writing, and teaching, my knowledge of women's psychological development advanced to a point where I considered myself somewhat of an expert on the midlife transition, especially in women. It is not a topic that many people show any interest in, but this knowledge has helped me come to terms with my own quest to become an authentic person and allows me to help women who find themselves feeling different and ostracized from other Christian women. This difference usually stems from the fact that they are not comfortable playing the traditional role dictated by society and by their dominant subculture, the church.

9. Jung, *Two Essays*, 174.

10. Hall and Nordby, *A Primer of Jungian Psychology*, 34.

9

Reinterpreting Women's Roles

What we were attempting after all was a total reversal not only of history and its public traditions but also of the daily life in which we were immersed. For that we needed super-female strength, the courage to face the size of the task, and the minute-to-minute persistence to do it over and over and over again in the face of threats and beseechings and naggings and clear statements of the impossibility of the whole undertaking, which after all have not ceased yet. We needed heroines and saints, not just role models.[1]

THROUGHOUT MY PUBLIC SCHOOL and early college education, I was one of those students who felt history was dry and unimportant to our everyday lives. Being an extremely practical person, I could not see how something that happened decades or centuries earlier had anything to do with my life. A couple of things helped me change my mind. First, we moved to New England where historical events and significant forefathers are documented at each turn in the road. Every time a friend or relative came from the South to visit us, Gary gave them a tour through New England, and I learned along with the visitors.

An even stronger force in teaching me the value of history was my graduate studies. The field of human development draws from many disciplines: psychology, sociology, philosophy, and history. In the 1980s, when I returned to graduate school, women's biographies and history books became a new fascination for me. Unexpectedly, these history lessons contributed enormously to my understanding of my own development process. Had I attempted to use history earlier in my life to understand myself, it would have been a wasted endeavor because there were few women's history books and biographies until after the women's

1. Janeway, *Cross Sections from a Decade of Change*, 15.

movement. In the 1970s, they began to emerge from every corner of the Western world, and a broader sampling of women's lives told us that women were not as one-dimensional as previously thought. A rich female legacy makes it possible for us today to go outside the traditional, nurturing-only norm.

One of the most significant lessons I learned from history was how important cohort—that is, the times in which we live—is to the role we play in society. For example, World War II had a tremendous influence on women's roles, not just during the war, but ever since. Because I was born during World War II and was a member of one of the last cohorts of women to be socialized to be housewives only, that historical tidbit was a treasure in understanding my own need to do something noteworthy outside the home. My dad's experience in the war and what he taught me about people outside our little corner of the world in Colorado set the stage for me to "get out there," explore, and create a better world.

Another important lesson I learned from history was that no time period stands alone. Although I had always heard the phrase "history repeats itself," I had no idea what that truly meant until I began to study women's roles in society. What happened to young girls and women in the 1950s and early 1960s was not a new phenomenon. The social norms dominant then were a repeat of earlier times, in particular, the early 1800s when a new ideology, referred to as *separate spheres*, arose to make women feel more comfortable with their stay-at-home role. The term *separate spheres* referred to the division in realms inhabited by men and women. Men were to dominate the public realm, which was outside the home, such as the world of work, politics, and community leadership; women were to take the lead in the private realm, the home and all activities that nurtured the family.[2] The private sphere of women was also referred to as the "proper sphere" or "the angel in the house."[3] Consequently, while masculine identity became associated with the world outside the home, a woman's identity came from creating and maintaining a haven for men as they came in from the cold, materialistic, dog-eat-dog world.

2. Bose, "Dual Spheres," in Hess and Ferree, *Analyzing Gender*.

3. Ross, "Separate Spheres or Shared Dominions?" 229.

THE CULT OF DOMESTICITY

During the development of industrial capitalism in the United States, men left the home to work instead of living in a family economy where all members of the family worked together. Women were left at home in a separate sphere with only a vaguely defined role. The relationship between husband and wife and parents and children changed drastically. A man's ability to earn money became a symbol of his worth; wealth became a sign of individual success. Women, then, had the primary parenting responsibility and the edict to make the house a home: "to shelter and rest man, as husband and father, after his day's work in the world."[4] With this clear division between the sexes came an organized attempt to keep women in their designated place, known as the Cult of True Womanhood, but relabeled by many modern sociologists as the Cult of Domesticity.[5] This ideology empowered women within the home sphere, giving them rules to live by. The purpose of this effort apparently was to address the unmet needs of women, to make them feel that their role in society was important, but a less-publicized goal was to keep women at home in their designated place.

The primary proponent of the Cult of True Womanhood was Catharine Beecher, who helped found several women's colleges in the Midwest in the 1840s and 1850s before she wrote *A Treatise on Domestic Economy*, the book that launched this movement.[6] The mundane work of running a household was downplayed, and the more fulfilling duties of educating children and caring for the emotional needs of the family were glorified. Catharine Beecher was a wealthy woman, and what she proposed could become reality only among women who had domestic servants to take care of much of the daily routine work. Home economics as a college degree emerged during this period. Women were to learn to be experts in domestic science. Of course, only a very few were able to go to college, and the people who needed the knowledge the most—the poorer women—could not afford it.

4. Matthaei, *An Economic History*, 109. See also Rothman, *Woman's Proper Place*.

5. Welter, "The Cult of True Womanhood."

6. This was first published in 1841. Beecher also wrote "The Duty of American Women to Their Country" (1845), and "Common Sense Applied to Religion" (1857), and, with her sister, Harriet Beecher Stowe, "The American Woman's Home" (1869). Harriet Beecher Stowe was the author of *Uncle Tom's Cabin*. Their brother, Henry Ward Beecher, was a famous orator and prominent minister. His most well-known assignment was Plymouth Church in Brooklyn. Along with his sisters, he supported women's suffrage.

With the advent of the Cult of True Womanhood, the inequality among different classes of women became more pronounced, as it did among their children. Children of the middle and upper classes were made more and more dependent on their mothers, while children in poor families were still working in terribly undesirable conditions. Middle-class mothers came to believe that they were responsible for how their children turned out, which is a two-edged sword. They were praised if the children were good and blamed if something went wrong. Other influences, such as the father's absence and the social milieu, were discounted. Theoretically, the interests and needs of both men and women were met in this new family system, but, gradually, many men became overly involved in their provider role and women preoccupied with housework and children. Gender roles were out of balance. The first women's movement in the 1840s attempted to address this need for change. Because it followed so closely on the heels of the antislavery movement, empowered, educated women who were already involved in abolition became more adamant about correcting the inequities between men and women. But as soon as women began to seek their rights, counteractions began, set in motion by conservative politicians and Christians.

THE CULT OF DOMESTICITY
AND THE CHRISTIAN SUBCULTURE

In the late 1970s, when I first began to question my traditional role as a Christian woman, I was completely unaware of the historical context of the denomination to which I belonged. Because my husband was obtaining a PhD in early church history and was a serious student of New Testament Greek, I had always left the decisions regarding our religious beliefs to him. I felt unintelligent and inarticulate next to him and other graduate students who passed through our lives. But when I became deeply entrenched in my own study of human development, I acquired the skills and found the courage to question what I had been taught.

It took ten years to complete my graduate work in human development, and then I began my own study of history. By then, it was the mid 1990s, and women's history books and biographies were plentiful. Finally, I had access to the information I had always craved. As I devoured these books, a few more pieces in the puzzle of the interpretation of women's lives fell into place. A big piece, however, was still missing:

Since women's development and their contributions to society had been ignored for hundreds of years and there appeared to be little understanding of woman's true nature, was it possible that women's role in the church had also been misinterpreted? I was beginning to see a pattern in society. When women attempted to leave the home and step a little into the public realm, countless men and women alike reacted strongly in an attempt to preserve the world as they had always known it. They became quite outspoken, both orally and through the written word, attempting to keep the status quo between the genders.

From my study of the first women's movement in the mid 1800s, I discovered that those who were the most adamantly against women's rights were the religious leaders and fervent Christians, both male and female. A good example of a non-traditional woman being ostracized by Christians was Abby Kelley, a Quaker who, after much introspection and prayer, decided that her calling was public speaking. Abby was a passionate speaker, so men and women alike attended her sessions, "spellbound by her firsthand account of slavery, impatient with the slightest noise which might cause the loss of a word."[7] However, there was a backlash against her, led by church leaders:

> Church leaders who had never taken a strong stand against slavery and had resisted demands to sever ties with Protestant denominations in the South now saw thousands of their members converted to radical antislavery by two women who were lecturing in bold defiance of the doctrines of St. Paul. Women were the backbone of the church, making up the bulk of the congregation on Sundays, depositing their pennies in mite boxes to support missionaries, sewing clothing for needy theological students. There was a clear and present danger that they might desert church circles for antislavery work. Already the Lynn [Mass.] Female Society had resolved at its annual meeting, "That while we hold two millions and a half of our countrymen in slavery, and shut them out from the light of the gospel, it is inconsistent for us to lend our aid to any foreign mission."[8]

Well-established newspapers also ridiculed women speakers, trying to discourage them from continuing:

7. Sterling, *Ahead of her Time*, 53.
8. Ibid.

The New York papers "poked fun at 'the Amazonian farce.' . . . "The spinster has thrown aside her distaff—the blooming beauty her guitar—the matron her darning needle—the sweet novelist her crow-quill; the young mother has left her baby to nestle alone in the cradle—and the kitchen maid her pots and frying pans—to discuss the weightier matters of state—to decide upon intricate questions of international policy."[9]

A similar reaction occurred in the 1970s and 1980s as a backlash to the twentieth-century women's movement. When women in broader society began to achieve more rights legally, those who felt threatened by these rights began a campaign to discredit the feminist movement. The books of Helen Andelin in the 1970s extol the "perfect woman." Even in the twenty-first century, I encountered similar advice by Andelin on her Web site. Calling her concept the "Fascinating Way," she discussed a fictional television drama that "glorifies the housewife, not the career woman."[10] According to her, the ideal woman is:

Feminine, domestic, an ideal woman from a man's point of view—kind, serving, caring, with longsuffering patience and a strong moral character, yet with a human side too—feminine and refined, sparkling and childlike, not easily pushed around—the kind of woman men adore. . . .[11]

On this Web site, she gave a list of the "accomplishments" of the feminist movement with comments on how women can better serve in their traditional role in the home:

If women have been unhappy with their role in the home it is because they have not given enough to it. If we merely feed and clothe children and keep the house clean we are "unprofitable servants," deserving neither thanks nor reward.

Women of the movement feel they must leave their meager roles in the home to serve humanity elsewhere. They must find a cure for cancer or serve in science, industry or the government. They ignore the fact that they can best serve society in the home, preparing their children to be useful citizens, instilling in them moral values, inspiring them to noble goals and serving as their husband's support in an increasingly threatening world.

9. Ibid., 50.

10. Andelin, *Marriage, the Fascinating Way* Web site.

11. Ibid.

The feminists have rejected their feminine sphere, where they are so desperately needed and are forcing their way into the man's world, thinking it is a better place. Here they must compete with men for equality. Here they must strive for position, taking on the traits of aggressiveness and determination if they are to succeed along with men. But women, if they are truly women, will never excel men in his world, unless they lose their womanliness. They will be misfits, wandering between two worlds but excelling in neither.

There is no justification for women to desert their posts in the home and offer to help men solve their problems. Women have had a record of failure in the home. Most of our social problems stem from homes where the woman has failed to establish a successful home life. We have an alarmingly high record of divorce, family turmoil and youth problems. Isn't it presumptuous on the part of women to leave their homes, where they have failed, and offer to help men solve their problems? The weak spot in America is the home—where the emphasis should be in solving problems.[12]

After first reading Andelin, I remember truly understanding what the old saying "ignorance is bliss" meant. I had spent the past twenty years trying to comprehend the complexity of our society and gender roles, and it was extremely frustrating to hear someone boil it down to one source: feminists. But frustration always serves a useful purpose. It makes us ask better questions and look deeper for answers. I was beginning to see what it was about the traditional teachings on women's roles that was causing my irritation. They were quite one-sided; all women had to be alike, especially Christian women. Perhaps it was time for a new look at exactly what a Christian wife of today should be. What do we mean by the term, "Christian wife," "Godly woman," or a "glorious woman"? That meant digging deep into the Scriptures and early church history to understand first what Paul was speaking of when he penned the words that have kept women in a subordinate position to men for centuries.

WOMEN'S ROLES IN THE CHURCH AND HOME

Consequently, I began to study more seriously the role of women in the Scriptures. Meeting weekly with two other Christian women, we scanned most of the New Testament looking closely for confirmation

12. Ibid.

that women truly must be in a subordinate role in the church and home. From a quick reading of the gospels, it seemed that Jesus' teachings freed women from the subservient role found in the Old Testament and Jewish literature. Women were considered equal in most respects. Although the apostles were all males, many of Jesus' disciples and faithful followers were women. Some even had participated quite responsibly in Jesus' ministry. Jesus' teachings and interactions with women reflect none of the religious or cultural gender hierarchy found in the first century. He mixed freely and naturally with women. He treated women as worthy individuals, not as a separate class of people. Jesus even entrusted testimony of the most important event of his life on earth—his resurrection—to a woman.[13] The bottom line appeared to be that Jesus treated women equally. There is no hint of hierarchy in the gospels other than the selection of men only for apostles. Was this simply a reflection of culture, or was there another reason women were excluded? Was it just not a good time in history to place women in leadership roles, since the social norms of the times kept women in the background, or did God truly want women to be in a subordinate role? The next step was to study Paul's writings.

As I read and reread the familiar writings by Paul and Peter[14] about women being submissive, and saw how men were also clearly told to be submissive, I became more confused and somewhat suspicious of why women had been kept in a subordinate role and how men had been interpreting the Scriptures such that they could justify keeping women in their place. I was beginning to realize that some men used the Scriptures to rationalize harmful treatment of women, including manipulation, denigration, and even abuse. During this time, I had become a volunteer in a shelter for women who were being abused by their husbands and was surprised at the spiritual element in many of these women's lives. Even men who were active, churchgoing Christians were physically and emotionally abusive to their wives. I realized the extent of the abuse of women and children in Christian homes following events in our own congregation and through involvement in a Christian organization that focused on awareness of domestic violence in Christian homes.[15] I felt I

---

13. Matt 27–28, Mark 15–16.

14. 1 Cor 11:2–16, Eph 5:21–33, Col 3:18–19, 1 Tim 2, 1 Pet. 3:1–12.

15. Peace and Safety in Christian Homes (PASCH). The president of this organization, Catherine Clark Kroeger, a longtime friend who introduced me to this organization. Much of her writing focused on the role of submission in the abuse of Christian women.

could no longer remain in the background. I became more vocal on the topic of submission and husband/wife relationships.

As I was becoming deeply interested in this topic, my husband revived his interest and began researching the Scriptures on submission. He admitted that he had questioned our traditional interpretations for many years, but had not had the time to complete an in-depth study of the issues. The more we studied, from our two different perspectives, the closer we came in our interpretation of what those early teachings meant to us today. I was looking at the issue from the social and historical perspective, while he was reading the original Greek and reviewing articles and books on what theologians had to say on the topic. Our uncertainties were becoming more similar, and we could, at least, have an open discussion about the topic. In the 1990s, Gary taught a class in our church on women's praying in the assembly. This began a dialogue about women's roles in the church that would continue for several years. For the most part, our fellow Christians were agreeing that a new interpretation of the Scriptures was needed.

CHURCH LEADERS' INVOLVEMENT

Church leaders must do more than talk. A process must be in place that allows needed changes to be made. In our particular denomination, local church leaders have the authority to make these changes in principle and practice at the congregational level. Therefore, women gradually assumed leadership of service groups and were making decisions about church activities, but the worship service still was led entirely by men. The process that evolved was to first have the elders study a specific woman's issue: praying in public. Then, Bible classes were taught on the related Scriptures so that anyone who was interested could study the topic. After the study, the elders made a decision to take the next step in their process and solicit feedback from members to see where everyone stood. With only a few exceptions, our members saw no problem with women praying in the worship service. Finally, the format of the worship service was altered to offer an opportunity for women to pray in public. A big step had been taken, but these women still were not leading a prayer. They were expressing, from their seats, their prayerful thoughts. Equality had not been reached, but the process was in place to achieve equality eventually.

After the initial, cautious beginning, a few years later, the elders began to receive requests from individual women to be even more involved in the worship service. They decided it was time for a comprehensive approach of studying women's roles in the church. In this extended process, the elders completed a biblical study among themselves to identify where they agreed and where they needed further study. They looked at all Scriptures related to women's roles in the church. Then, they offered a Bible class for individuals who were interested in studying the topic. Gary led an intensive study that included relevant Bible passages, early church history, and current evangelical interpretations of these Scriptures. Members of the class were polled after the study to determine where they stood on the topic. Then, the elders met and discussed the next step, which culminated in a statement that indicated their viewpoint.[16] Using this statement as a talking point, the elders met with each member of the congregation and asked for their input. Did they agree with the statement? Should we put it into practice in the near future? If you disagree, would it hinder you from worshipping with us? A very small number of members disagreed with the statement.[17] Further study was offered for the few people who asked for it, and the next step in the process—training and guiding of all people who participate in the worship service—was initiated.[18]

As I complete the writing and editing of this book, this decision-making process is nearing its completion. I am attempting to interpret

16. The statement read: "For some time the Elders have been studying this issue of women's roles. Through the course of our study we have come to a unified agreement that as far as God is concerned there is no distinction between what a man or a woman may do in any gathering of [this church]." Further clarification indicated that these functions were included in the statement: Scripture reading, prayer, communion thought, worship coordinator, song leader, teaching of adult Bible classes, and preaching.

17. During this process, one 94-year-old African American widow who had worshipped with us for many years said, "What about the passage that says, 'Women are to keep silent in the church'"? The elders explained to her that, in that passage, Paul was addressing a specific abuse of a limited group of wives in Corinth. It is wrong to remove that verse from its context and apply it to all women in every setting for all times. Her face lit up with a smile of relief. She said that recently she had reread that verse and wanted to ask one of the elders what it meant. The way it had always been explained to her, and had been used to silence her, had never made sense. She thanked the elders for answering one of her lifelong questions.

18. A larger church that has policy dictated from a national or international organization would, of course, have to follow a different approach, but in this small fellowship, the process worked to bring about more equality.

what this step means for me. I have been in a dialogue with my husband on this topic for years, wanting women to have equality in the church. But, at this point, in spite of my role as a teacher in a public university and responsible work in the corporate world, I cannot imagine me being involved in a leadership role in the church. When one remains for many years in a subordinate role, it is extremely difficult to take the first step out of that role. To help make that transition, I am reevaluating where I have been and where I would like to go next. Even though I had frequent negative thoughts regarding the church, my relationship with my husband has improved to the point that I no longer feel as negative about the subject. I have reached this point because of the relationship I now have with Gary. From the beginning of our marriage, our relationship did not suffer, because my husband never demanded submission. Our relationship was more of a partnership in most respects. On the home front, I had all the independence I needed. I had been a joint breadwinner with my husband for years. We had joint responsibility for financial management and decision making in our household. My primary frustration with our relationship was our inability to discuss freely theological and church practice issues. Because he had become more willing to listen and discuss these issues, and we realized how few differences we really had, my frustration had lessened considerably.

So, where did this leave me in my long venture of making sense of my life? With this process in place, I still felt the need to fill in the gaps in my knowledge regarding women's roles in the church. How did we get to this point? I felt I must continue my research on women's history and gender roles in society. To be more effective in working with others, I had to make sure that I had my own questions answered.

WOMEN'S HISTORY

For the past decade, my primary path for determining "the truth" has been through the study of history. Since I had neglected this segment of my education previously, I had a daunting task ahead. Through the reading of biographies and history books, I began my study with the nineteenth century and worked backwards. The parallels between the nineteenth and twentieth centuries became clearer. Beginning in the 1840s with the first women's movement, women gradually became more involved in activities outside the home, especially in public speaking roles. That automatically led Christian women to question their own silence in the church and submissiveness in the home. I was amazed to discover that the topic of women's roles in the church had been visited repeatedly throughout Western history. Some of the women who had taken the path less traveled, the one that led away from being a traditional wife and mother, became my role models.

Lucretia Mott headed my list of mentors. A strong Quaker, she was involved alongside her husband in the peace movement just prior to the Civil War. She began to speak to women along the East Coast on women's roles in society. Lucretia's childhood experiences had prepared her to take on this public role. Her biography told of several pivotal events in her development. She was born in 1793, a time of rapid change in the philosophy and belief systems that influenced the men and women in prominent positions in society.

> Had she been raised anywhere but on Nantucket, she might have remained obscure. But the life of the island, giving women a great deal of responsibility, plus the belief of Quakerism, the dominant religion, that men and women are equal, created a climate in which a woman could find her way. Mary Starbuck, a collateral ancestor of Lucretia's, was known as the Great Woman for her role in the early governance of the island. Maria Mitchell, a cousin, was the nation's first woman astronomer.[19]

On one occasion, while visiting Nantucket, Lucretia witnessed a horrible incident that influenced her for the rest of her life:

> On the town square a crowd had gathered to watch a woman being whipped at the public whipping post. The little girl did not learn her crime, or promptly forgot it, but indignation over the whipping flared within her. Seventy-five years later she led grandchildren and great-grandchildren to the spot where the whipping post had been and told them in a trembling voice how angry it had made her.[20]

Also in Nantucket, Lucretia met Elizabeth Coggeshall, who inspired her to become a public speaker. She described her mentor as

> a married women of thirty-three with such a gift in the ministry that her own Meeting released her to travel and preach at other Meetings. Such men and women were known as Public Friends. If the Public Friend was a woman, members of the family took

19. Bacon, *Valiant Friend*, 9.
20. Ibid., 11.

care of her household and children so that she could follow her leading. Four years earlier Elizabeth Coggeshall had made an extensive trip to England. Lucretia stood in awe of her. To be a Public Friend, to travel and be listened to, to what higher calling could a Quaker girl aspire?"[21]

Lucretia did not immediately become a public speaker upon reaching adulthood; she had to wait until the time was right. So she went on with her life, getting married and having children like other women of her time. The events that led up to the Civil War offered Lucretia and her husband the opportunity to become involved in a peace movement. Because Lucretia was a wife and mother of five children and had a husband who supported her public activities, she became a role model for a generation of women who acquired an education and wanted to use it outside the home.

I discovered numerous similarities between nineteenth-century women ministers and public speakers on human rights issues and the twentieth century of my upbringing, but one was dominant: All feminists were lumped together by their opponents as marriage and family destroyers. They were accused of propagating a philosophy that would destroy the family as we have always known it. Opponents reinforced the idea that the traditional way was the only Scriptural way for marriage and family to function. Most people I encountered bought into the idea that the women's movement was harmful to our society and should be discredited. I had once been of the same mind. At the time, my decision regarding the subject was based on practically no firsthand knowledge of what feminists really stood for. It took me many years to put it all together, to see how I had accepted teachings based on personal biases and uneducated guesses. For example, I was naive and uninformed enough to believe that all the men and women qualified to preach and teach in our churches and publish books through our Christian publishers were "credentialed" and had the right to speak out.

For women to change their roles, men had to do the same. When men were at home, they needed to share responsibility for household chores. The most prevalent issue was childcare. How could women work outside the home and take care of their children? It was assumed by traditionalists that the children would have to take care of themselves. But, on the other side of the issue, historians and sociologists pointed

21. Ibid., 16.

out that minority, working-class, and poor women had always worked outside the home. African American women had a long history of being successful in both spheres. How could we label these determined women who had both careers and families as bad mothers? Learning from other cultures was not yet something that the average middle-class, white American considered. Only historians and sociologists were aware of how narrow our interpretation of women's lives had been. The push for equality on one side and the determination to keep the status quo on the other set up a culture clash.

CLASH OF CULTURES

The clash of cultures in our society was the primary source of my own confusion and unhappiness. Having been brought up in a world where nearly all women stayed at home after they had children contributed more than I knew at the time to my feelings of conflict. My parents did not deliberately instill that message in me, but I was surrounded by examples of it. I began to understand this more from my own parenting role. As my children left home to form their own homes and identities, I noticed that they were more likely to do what we did than what we said. The same was true when I attempted to interpret my feelings and actions regarding women's roles. What women were doing, not what they were saying, created in me a subconscious belief that women truly were subordinate. Yet what I was hearing from the media and academia during these changing times was the opposite.

It was the contradiction between my childhood socialization and the world I was living in as an adult, not individual people in my immediate surroundings, that was tormenting me. On one hand, I had been taught that women, like children, were to be seen, not heard. Even in my mother's extended family, which consisted of five sisters and no brothers, the men dominated. My grandfather, the husbands of my mother's sisters, and, later, grandsons were catered to and never contradicted in public—though I heard quite a few snide remarks when the "girls" were by themselves. At holiday meals, the men and children ate dinner first, then the women. I probably absorbed a lot of "truths" from those all-female sessions that later colored my interpretation of relationships between men and women.

My mother also attempted to instill in me the need not to talk too much, especially around men. That message influenced my inability to speak out in church settings for most of my life. The message was rein-forced by the fact that men only were speaking in public church services. Even today, as I sit in Bible classes, I notice that very few women talk. We listen as men go into long discussions about a particular Scripture, but we seldom speak up. Many women sit quietly, doodle, or write (as I did earlier). It is amazing how much that message to be silent was un-consciously stamped on my mind and, evidently, on the minds of other women.

In addition to general observations about interactions between men and women, I heard, as a child, sermons on the husband/wife rela-tionship and woman's place being in the home. Women were to be sub-missive, not speak in public, and not "usurp authority over men" (that sounded pretty lethal, though I doubt I understood what it meant).

As a young adult in the 1970s and 1980s, although unaware of the academic research being conducted on the gender issues, I began to hear and read about the new society where women were equal, just as intelli-gent as men, and capable of doing what men had always done. However, this new knowledge was not compatible with what I was hearing in our churches, where men were in control of both the public and the private spheres. The argument I heard to justify this arrangement was that we were to follow what the Bible taught—but the Bible is silent on many of the issues that men presented as scriptural. I believe most men and women honestly felt they were following the Scriptures when, in fact, might have been unconsciously following deeply entrenched societal traditions.

Seeing present-day struggles in the context of history, I became more convinced that social norms and trends, not the Scriptures, were forcing women to remain in their traditional roles. Bonnie Miller-McLemore, an academic Christian author, confirmed this view.[22] In our own church's literature, more objective views on women's roles were emerging. A new question arose in my mind: How could women have gained so much ground in the nineteenth century and then fallen back into traditional roles in the twentieth century? We had taken a few steps forward, but several more back.

Although my husband and I had unresolved issues, our beliefs were merging. We were discovering together and discussing openly these un-answered questions regarding the contradictions between early church

---

22. Miller-McLemore, *Also a Mother*.

teachings and our twentieth-century interpretations. Gary led the congregational process of studying the Scriptures thoroughly and deciding on a change in policy regarding women's participation in worship. Now, what remains is for us to work together to train and guide women to feel comfortable and to become involved in the worship service. Because of our teaching and training experience, we need to take the lead in the ongoing changes in our own congregation. Women will need mentors and men guidance as they see their wives taking a more public position. Therefore, in addition to helping couples resolve issues in their marriage, Gary and I must take a more active role in helping them see that God's initial purpose for men and women was to minister together. As I wrote in one memo to myself:

> Perhaps God's purpose for us is to teach others not only the fundamentals of living a Christian life, but the techniques of forming and maintaining a Christian marriage in a world that has changed drastically from the Christian couple that the New Testament is defining, a life where the woman has taken on a completely different role in the world outside the church. . . . Through our Christian marriage and genuine concern for each other and for our children, we can help disprove some of the traditions in the church that give women no place in this modern world.

This sounds exactly like I am writing another happy ending, but it is not a new one. I wrote this ending to a memo in 1979, when I was on the quest to make sense out of my life. It took another thirty years to reach a point where it could become a reality.

10

God's Plans for Husbands and Wives

B ECAUSE GARY IS A church leader, and because our marriage has lasted nearly fifty years, we are often asked to meet with couples who are having marital problems. During these sessions, one of us mentions the Scripture about how a husband is supposed to love his wife (Eph 5:25–28, Col 3:19). The husband automatically says, "I love her, but . . ." and goes on to discuss all her shortcomings and how she is not living up to what the Scriptures say a Christian wife should be. I immediately think about how freely we use the word "love," but really don't have a true picture of what it means. This was one of the first topics I studied when I was having trouble with my marriage in the 1970s. At the time, I was influenced heavily by the depictions of love in popular songs and movies.

WHAT IS LOVE?

Determining what love is by listening to popular music is like my grand-daughter learning how to be a girl by watching animated "princess" movies. Before she turned three years old, her idea of love was to sing romantic songs, get gooey-eyed, and snuggle with someone on the sofa. In my early adulthood, one of my favorite singers was Karen Carpenter, whose songs of love painted a picture quite similar to my granddaughter's interpretation. Love was a feeling of wanting to be physically close to someone. She sang of dreams coming true because of this closeness. A couple *in love* felt like angels were "sprinkling moon dust in your hair." At the time, after fifteen years of marriage, I was not seeing much moon dust in my relationship. I considered my husband to be my best friend, but was I "in love" with him? Were my feelings for him that much different than those I had for other people with whom I spent time? How could someone with a childhood like mine, where love was not discussed and emotions were not shown, recognize love when she saw it?

93

As I struggled with my marriage and with general discontent, I turned to music to relieve some of the internal turmoil. Music had always been a big part of my life. As an adolescent, I had spent a large segment of my discretionary time at the piano, but had neglected it after I married. Once the children were born and I was working full time, I gave it up completely. During my long crisis, music reentered my life as a deeply felt, urgent need. I listened, with passion, to the popular music of the times. One song that influenced me and helped me form a definition of love was "Wedding Song."[1] A biblical song, it speaks of the union of two spirits joined together in marriage, but one phrase haunted me: "As it was in the beginning, is now until the end, woman draws her life from man and gives it back again." What did it mean to "draw your life" from a man? And what was I to do in return? These words appeared to be just another way to live out the princess-fairy-tale story that has captivated so many young girls and women throughout history: A woman finds a prince, falls in love, gets married, and is happy ever after.

After a few years of marriage, I knew that my life was never going to be like a fairy tale. Love alone did not make a marriage. I could relate more to songs of despair. The Neil Diamond song "I Am, I Said" was my story. He talked about being lonely and "lost between two shores." I was in the middle of a crisis, terribly restless and unhappy, with no idea what to do next. So, once again, I decided to take a class at the university to help me answer my latest questions. In that class, I discovered the writings of Leo Buscaglia, who helped me explore the topic of love.

LEO BUSCAGLIA AND LOVE

When I was thirty-nine, I began to read Buscaglia's book called *Love*.[2] For the first time ever, I studied seriously what love is. Through the reaction papers I wrote for the class, I began to understand more about the nature of love and the problems I had in defining it in my own life:

> Buscaglia's phrase, "Love teaches a man to show what he is feeling," is powerful to me. Because my parents did not openly express love, and because I had no opportunity to have a close relationship with anyone as a child who did express and discuss love, many of my adult years have been spent in learning how to love and how to express my love to others.

1. Stookey, "Wedding Song (There Is Love)."
2. Buscaglia also wrote a similar book, *Living, Loving, and Learning*.

Another of Buscaglia's insights that was particularly meaningful to me was the idea that love is a process. "Love is a process of building upon what is already there. Love is never complete in any person. There is always room for growth." Process automatically assumes change and growth, which is a complementary theme throughout the book *Love*. Without change, man is never likely to grow emotionally or mentally, perhaps even physically. Often, people who find themselves in a stagnant point in life, I believe, are actually craving a meaningful love relationship, even though the signs or symptoms emerge as burnout with a career, physical fatigue, other health problems, or even emotional or physical abuse of family members or close acquaintances.

These essays about love were autobiographical. What I wrote seems like common sense now, but, at the time, the ideas were novel. I finally had the opportunity to explore in depth the meaning of the word *love*.

Man needs to have at least "one person who cares deeply"; man has the need for "togetherness and love which become the major drive and goal of an individual's life."

I concluded that his application to man should be broadened to include women:

She needs, in order to be totally free to self-actualize, an understanding and supportive relationship with some *one* significant person. . . . If a person has one or more sound love relationships, he or she will feel free to choose his "own paths," to be adventuresome and creative, to be unique, because the love has given him or her the strength to be different.

I was beginning to see why I was "stuck" in my development. I could not focus on what to *do* with my life until I had developed a sound, open relationship with someone, and this someone needed to be my husband. I had to be able to tell my husband what I felt about everything, including what I thought about the church around which our whole life revolved. To feel comfortable telling him my thoughts was impossible, because I felt he disapproved of me when I did not agree with or think like him. The underlying questions that had to be answered were: Did I love my husband? and did he love me?

Not only did I question my love for Gary; I also questioned his love for me. It was obvious that he did not approve of some of my ideas and habits. And, when I tried to talk about my feelings, he did not want to discuss them. He said we should wait until I was "rational" to discuss the topic. But, once I had my emotional outburst, I was through with the topic. Ultimately, after each disagreement, we would quietly go on as we always had, so our relationship remained terribly strained. Gary made me feel insignificant and unintelligent, not because he used those words, but because he questioned my ability to reason as he could. He made me feel like I was the weak person with problems; he was the strong, "perfect" one. We were at an impasse, and neither of us wanted to reopen the issue because of the devastating feelings that resulted.

Because of our Christian upbringing and strong commitment to remain in a marriage regardless of how we felt about each other, we continued to follow what we believed the Scriptures taught.

A WIFE'S LOVE

A Christian, regardless of marital status, has the command from God to "love one another." Countless Scriptures tell us this. A few years back, I went through the New Testament and gathered together all the Scriptures I could find about loving one another. I completed this task because it seemed so obvious that any person who is a Christian should automatically know how to treat his or her spouse. The submission decree would take back seat if we would simply follow the underlying theme of the New Testament: love one another. I was amazed at the number of Scriptures instructing us to love others.[3] In Romans 12:10, some clarifying words appear: We are to be "devoted" to one another and "honor" one another above ourselves. In Romans 15:7, we are told to "accept one another." Then, in 1 Corinthians 1:10 and Philippians 4:2, we are instructed to "agree with one another." In Galatians 5:13, we should "serve one another in love." And then, in the most well-known of Scriptures regarding men's and women's relationships, Ephesians 5:21 says we should "submit to one another out of reverence for Christ." James 4:11 says we should not "slander one another," and 1 Peter 3:8 says to "live in harmony with one another." Another Scripture that applies so appropriately to marriage is Galatians 6:2: "Carry each other's burdens, and in this way you will fulfill the law of Christ."

---

3. E.g., John 13:34, 1 Pet 1:22, 1 John 3:11, Rom 13:8.

These Scriptures give the basic foundation for a Christian wife to love her husband. She should, at the least, honor him, accept him, be devoted to him, carry his burden, and live in harmony with him. If a woman follows these commands, she will then, I suspect, be following God's plan to be in submission to her husband. It does not, however, mean that she must allow her husband to manipulate, denigrate, verbally abuse, or physically abuse her. If he is a Christian also, there is no reason why he would ever consider treating her so negatively. It is a win/win situation if both spouses are Christians and both follow the general commandments of the New Testament to love one another. But, sadly, we are all human and often forget to follow these commands.

From my study, and from the way my husband has interpreted the "submission" Scriptures, the burden of creating and maintaining a loving relationship lies with the husband. If a husband truly loves his wife and treats her accordingly, she will have little trouble following God's laws.

A HUSBAND'S LOVE

Regardless of my emotional state or my behavior toward Gary, he adhered faithfully to his religious belief that a husband is to love his wife. From the beginning of our relationship, he treated me with respect and love. His role model truly was Christ. If one reads Ephesians carefully, there is no excuse for treating any person badly. In chapter 4, Paul gives us elaborate details about how to live a Christian life:

> Be angry but do not sin; do not let the sun go down on your anger, and do not make room for the devil. . . . Let no evil talk come out of your mouths, but only what is useful for building up, as there is need, so that your words may give grace to those who hear. . . . Put away from you all bitterness and wrath and anger and wrangling and slander together with all malice, and be kind to one another, tenderhearted, forgiving one another. (Eph 4:26–32)

Without reading any further, a man and woman should know how to treat each other. But then, Paul makes it crystal clear: Women are to be in submission to their husbands and men are to love their wives and treat them accordingly. More specifically, they are told to "love your wives as Christ loved the church." Christian men are to follow Christ's example, not their earthly role models, as so often is the case. They are to be "imitators of Christ:"

> Husbands, love your wives, just as Christ loved the church and gave himself up for her, in order to make her holy by cleansing her with the washing of water by the word, so as to present the church to himself in splendor, without a spot or wrinkle or anything of the kind—yes, so that she may be holy and without blemish. In the same way, husbands should love their wives as they do their own bodies. He who loves his wife loves himself. For no one ever hates his own body, but he nourishes and tenderly cares for it, just as Christ does for the church , because we are members of his body. For this reason a man will leave his father and mother and be joined to his wife, and the two will become one flesh. This is a great mystery, and I am applying it to Christ and the church. Each of you, however, should love his wife as himself, and a wife should respect her husband. (Eph 5:21–33)

In this one passage, husbands are told three times to love their wives. The same admonition is also found in 1 Peter 3 and in Colossians 3. I cannot remember us actually discussing these passages until we had been married more than thirty years. I later discovered that Gary had for over forty years felt that the traditional interpretation of these Scriptures was not correct, but he would not discuss it because he had not studied it carefully enough to venture an opinion.

Because Gary's actions reflected his beliefs on this subject, that a husband must consistently and unconditionally love his wife, there was no basis for me to claim he did not love me. The questioning of my love for him and wondering if he loved me was not something we discussed. It was something I wondered about because his actions did not coincide with my childlike definition of love. I was not *feeling* loved at all times, and I did not always feel loving toward him. But he continued to treat me with respect and patiently did things for me that he thought would make me happy. His unwavering dedication to me was what pulled our marriage through. It is next to impossible to stay angry at a person who responds to negative comments with love and respect. Perhaps Paul and Peter knew that when they penned their letters.

Unfortunately, I did not use the Scriptures as my model for how to treat a husband. Instead I followed my female legacy—my mother and my grandmother were my teachers, and their behavior toward their husbands could not be labeled *loving*. My dad was much like my husband. He treated my mother with respect and love in spite of her moodiness and sharp tongue. I remember the only spanking I ever received from my dad was because I was "talking back to" my mother. I was seventeen years old, and he put me over his legs and spanked me, but he also soft-ened the blow by admitting that he did not know why my mother acted as she did. But, regardless, I was to show her respect. Common wisdom tells women that we choose husbands like our fathers, and, in my case, that was one of the smartest decisions I made. I also have sons who are like my father and their father. They treat women with respect.

So why, during my years of questioning, did I not see clearly what was going on? There are several reasons. As mentioned before, our fam-ily life was so hectic that we seldom had time to talk about anything that was not urgent. Though urgency should not determine how we spend our time, it normally takes priority over deeper, more important issues. For example, work deadlines and scheduled meetings may not be as im-portant as time spent with a loved one, but in the real world, we must follow the rules of the organizations that help us meet our basic survival needs. In our family life, we scarcely had enough time for routine every-day activities, and so seldom had quality time together. Consequently, I felt neglected and did not have my need for friendship and quality communication satisfied.

As I look back to those times, I question why the topic of Christian marriage was so seldom mentioned in sermons or in Bible classes. I heard many more sermons on women's roles and women being submissive to their husbands than I ever heard presenting both sides of a Christian marriage. Actually, the phrase I remember hearing frequently was "sub-ject to," terminology that was not easily understood. When I was a child and worshipped in a church that used the King James Bible, I became accustomed to shutting out Bible teachings because the language was foreign to me; I continued this practice in early adulthood.

Because of the church's silence on the subject of marriage, I must have assumed that everyone else knew how to make their marriages work. Ministers did not talk about the subject, Bible school teachers did not teach on the subject, and women with whom I held informal chat sessions never mentioned any problems with their marriages. My hus-band was also quiet on the topic because he did not like conflict. When a woman does not understand the source of a problem in her life, she is most likely to blame herself, thinking she is the only woman with this problem. If she does not have a neutral, understanding party with whom to talk, she will continue to blame herself, keep silent, and find no solu-tion to her problem. This can have very serious consequences.

COMMITMENT OR DIVORCE?

When one's marriage relationship is not good, it is easy to believe that the grass is greener on the other side of the fence. Then, one may decide that ending the marriage will alleviate the unhappiness. Only if a person has a strong commitment to remain married will he or she survive this temptation. Because of the pressure we were living under, I occasionally had thoughts of running away, leaving behind all my problems and starting over. But, though we seldom discussed it, both my husband and I had an unwavering belief that divorce was not the answer for Christians. We interpreted these Scriptures literally—God intended for us to be married only once.

In addition to my commitment to one marriage, I believed that divorce was extremely harmful to children unless one or both of the parents were abusive. I knew our marriage was not bad enough that our children would be better off living with only one parent. During those years, I was vividly aware of what happens to children when their parents get a divorce; my brother had endured a nasty divorce and was not allowed, by his wife, to see the children.[4] Also, in the late 1960s, I read a book about the changing family that defined and openly approved of, for the first time in our society as far as I knew, alternative lifestyles such as open marriages, where couples swapped partners. The social movements of the 1960s were beginning to influence family life, in some ways positively, but in other ways quite negatively.

These ideas were too radical for me, and I maintained my belief in commitment to one marriage; therefore, I knew that my marriage had to be fixed before I could move on. How to do that became a major challenge. It would require something I felt very uncomfortable doing: confronting my husband. Again, Buscaglia's books helped me see the absolute necessity of working out my marital problems so I would be free to grow as a human being. From his writings, I began to see the need, even for self-sufficient people, to engage with others. I reflected on his writings in 1979:

> One concept particularly meaningful to me is the idea of how important "others" are to the development of self. This truth dawned upon me slowly, because of the self-sufficient nature of my personality. At one time, I truly felt there was nothing in life that I

4. This was before divorce laws prohibited such control by either one of the divorced parties.

couldn't handle alone, but, through a series of sound friendships, I discovered that life is much easier and more meaningful when we depend on others occasionally. An extremely self-sufficient person may never know the joy of personal growth gained through deep interpersonal relationships. In Buscaglia's words, "fully functioning persons recognize their need for others." Love and intimacy allow persons to reflect "their vast potentials," to "share them with others," and offer a "special opportunity for growth."

To find peace in my marriage while still nourishing my need for independence and self-actualization was going to be very difficult, if not impossible. As Jean Baker Miller tells us, these are opposing concepts, often referred to as the self/other conflict.[5] The question I was attempting to answer was becoming clearer: How could I become a whole person without destroying my marriage and family? I knew confrontation was necessary, but I was not comfortable in situations of conflict. I had spent my life up to that point avoiding conflict with my husband. Why? Conflict is never pleasant, and typically I would avoid it until I became angry. Then, I would feel guilty because I thought *good* Christian women would never disagree or argue with their husbands. Isn't that what "being submissive" meant? Also, being a "good girl" had been deeply instilled in me. One of my memos discussed this concept:

> A woman's acquisition of masks begins in childhood when those around her insist that she be a good little girl or a "little lady." But, how does she know what that means? There is no rule book that tells us what the traits of a little lady are or how one should act. From my own experience, I thought a little lady was, first of all, the opposite of a boy. She should not get dirty, play rough, climb trees, sit with her legs spread open, or talk loudly. She should, on the other hand, be sweet, walk instead of running, wear clean and feminine dresses, and do housework instead of outdoor chores. In addition, a good little girl should not talk too much because the men in her life might not like it, and she definitely should not be a tattletale. And why should a little girl be good and act like a lady? Because she will then grow up to be a good woman, someone that a man will want to marry and take care of.

When I wrote this paragraph, I was trying to pinpoint the exact origin of the idea that women must be perfect. Although the concept goes back many centuries, it has been kept alive more recently by books

5. Miller, *Toward a New Psychology of Women.*

written primarily by women. As mentioned previously, in the 1970s, Helen Andelin encouraged wives to be completely virtuous:

> The way to happiness for a woman is the perfection of her an-gelic side. As she develops a kind, gentle, sympathetic character, yet one with strength of will, womanly courage and a sense of responsibility, she will grow towards this inner happiness essen-tial to the ideal woman. Then, as she learns to understand men, filling a need in their lives and bringing them greater happiness, she in turn attains the virtues of acceptance, understanding and appreciation, which further add to her happiness.[6]

How can a woman follow such instructions and, at the same time, bring up negative thoughts in conversations with her husband? To engage in conflict with one's husband was definitely not "angelic," and, there-fore, usually not done. But when conflict is avoided, the undercurrent of discontent creates some of the masks we women have come to wear. It is not, however, a good method for creating a healthy relationship within a long-term marriage. The conflict below the surface begins to germinate and swell, eventually breaking out and sometimes causing irresolvable conflict, ending in an acrimonious divorce. For a marriage to survive and blossom requires that couples find a balance between what each wants for him- or herself and what the other needs. This difficult process may be referred to as *mutual submission.*

MUTUAL SUBMISSION

Mutual submission appears to be what Paul is speaking of in Ephesians 5:21–33. First, he says we (all Christians) should be "subject to one anoth-er out of reverence for Christ." Without reading any further, it becomes apparent that both partners should respect and submit to one another because they have a deep love for each other and for Christ. Paul makes it even clearer: "wives, be subject to your husbands as you are to the Lord" and "husbands, love your wives, just as Christ loved the church and gave himself up for her." First Peter 3:1–12 gives the same instructions. Wives are to accept the authority of their husbands, but it goes on to say how husbands are supposed to treat their wives: "show consideration for your wives, paying honor to the woman . . . so that nothing hinders your prayers." If you are married, to be the kind of Christian man or woman God intends you to be requires a continual practicing of mutual submis-

6. Andelin, *Fascinating Womanhood*, 126.

sion. Peter ends his discussion with another clear statement of how to treat one another: "Finally, all of you have unity of spirit, sympathy, love for one another, a tender heart, and a humble mind." Looking at these verses as a whole, how could any person believe the Scriptures allow a man to rule over or control a woman? This conclusion goes against the entire premise of the New Testament.

Putting these beliefs into practice and maintaining them day after day is not as simple as intellectualizing about them. The words are clear, but finding a way to bring this about so that each person in the relationship can live out at least some of his or her own goals and dreams requires a basic understanding of human behavior, knowledge of each other's needs, and accomplished communication skills. Obviously, this set of knowledge and skills does not just appear when one gets married; it takes many years of practice. To stay in the relationship until this level is reached requires commitment to the marriage and consciously working on skills and practices that strengthen the marriage.

Looking back over nearly fifty years of marriage, I remember how hard we worked to create a strong union. Little changes are important. Our drastically different personality and working styles led to many conflicts. For example, when we were a young couple with three small children, my husband worked part time because he was in graduate school, and I worked full time to help support the family. I had primary responsibility for the home and basic childcare, though he did what he could to lessen my load. One day, he suggested that we should not run out of basic supplies in the house (like toilet paper and soap), so I calmly told him that if he didn't want to run out of supplies, he could purchase them himself. From that day forward, he became the primary shopper in our family, and he loves doing it. He shops for bargains, and we have large quantities of all paper goods and basic staples for cooking. He shops, I cook. And, when he purchases too many things for our shelves, we donate them to the church's food pantry.

When we had little babies and diapers to wash (before disposables), he carried the diaper pail down to the washer each evening and put them in to soak. In the morning, I washed them. Sometime during the day, he dried them, and, in the evening after the children were in bed, I folded them. This seems like a small, unimportant thing, but in my mind, service was one of the most important ways he could show his love. We both had to learn not to expect perfection from each other.

Over the years, Gary was willing to help with the laundry, but I did not like his timing. I wanted the clothes washed on the weekend and ready to go when we began a new week. Because I complained, Gary stopped helping. Finally, he told me why he was not helping, and I had to change my standard.

One of my major complaints over the years was my lack of space for schoolwork and then teaching preparation. Gary had always had his own desk, but I had no place to spread out my papers and store my books. I was continually running up and down the stairs looking for books or supplies. In the 1990s, I took on a consulting role that required that I work at home. At that point, with more money of my own, I remodeled our daughter's old bedroom for a study of my own, alleviating my long-held frustration. We are currently revisiting that problem because we may soon each need our own desktop computer. At least, we are discussing the need openly.

After many years of working out little details in keeping the household functioning properly, we now have more defined roles. Basically, I am in charge of the house, and he the yard and home maintenance. But he also helps with regular household chores. I have learned that I must be the household manager. I would prefer that Gary initiate tasks inside the house, but he wants me to make a list and tell him what to do. So, I straighten, organize, and set priorities for him; Gary vacuums, mops, and makes small repairs. He does nearly all of the shopping except for clothing purchases. He offers to run errands for me and never complains when I ask for his help. We both do the laundry and empty or load the dishwasher. When one of us has a deadline at work, the other steps in to do more of the housework. On occasion, when we are both busy, we have to hire someone to help out with the cleaning and yard work; otherwise, a martyr syndrome (feeling sorry for ourselves) sets in. These little details are one major way we show our love for each other. Love, in our case, is more about action than words, but it has taken many decades to understand this fully and to implement the right actions.

PERSONAL GROWTH AND MARRIAGE

Personal growth and marriage might seem to be incompatible. Personal growth requires individual freedom to explore and experiment with options, while marriage requires continual sacrificing of one's own needs for another. How can these two opposing forces—self versus other—

ever arrive at a middle ground? Roger and Renee Gould attempted to address this issue in an unpublished paper that focuses on the "relationship between an individual's inherent need to grow and the difficulties and benefits that the actualization of that need brings to a marriage."[7] As a rule, growth in adulthood is measured by how well we achieve as an individual, though there is no doubt that the initial criteria for this assessment were based on the male model of development that has pervaded the social science literature for decades.[8] In other words, men were considered adults when they became independent, aggressive, and productive. Women were judged by their ability to help men accomplish these things. When our society changed and women were told they were equal with men, many decided they had the right to develop into their full potential. The obvious result was conflict.

According to the Goulds, between the ages of sixteen and fifty, we must master our childhood fears and learn to modulate childhood anger. Otherwise, we will never live up to our full adult potential. To reach this potential, then, we have to uncover layer after layer of buried childhood pain. The best place to do this is within an intimate, trusting relationship. That is why the marriage relationship is so vital to personal development, but it can also be damaging if each partner is not willing to allow the other to grow. This helped me understand the complexity of the marriage relationship, which, to truly succeed, must accommodate two childhood consciousnesses at varying stages of development at the beginning of the marriage. Once a couple is married, they are bombarded by elements outside the relationship: work pressures and relationships, extended family influences, community and church expectations, children, and both subtle and overt changes in society. Throw into this mix two sets of age-related developmental tasks, and we have a recipe for disaster. Marital issues simmer below the surface for years and then erupt in a form that makes no sense to either partner. What appeared to be a match made in heaven can turn into a nightmare.

In their writings, the Goulds focus on the developmental process of the two individuals within the relationship. They explore what happens when one partner initiates a necessary growth step and the other reacts negatively because he or she feels envy, jealousy, or fear. The emphasis

7. Gould and Gould, *Personal Growth and Marital Consequences*, 1.

8. See more about the male model in psychological growth in Miller, *New Psychology*; Fels, *Necessary Dreams*; and Gilligan and Brown, *Meeting at the Crossroads*.

here placed on *necessary growth* is vital. Often, when one partner grows in a different direction, the other sees it as a purposeful effort to upstage him or her. In reality, the growth is internally triggered, unconscious at the beginning of the process.

> This growth process is relentless! It refuses to stop when faced with the convention of marriage. When both partners in a marriage continue their individual growth patterns and allow or support the other, the marriage is healthy. When one partner *interferes* or is *seen to* interfere with the other's growth, the compact of good will becomes a compacted anger and loved ones become enemies.
>
> In each instance of a troubled marriage, there is an underlying dynamic of one person being threatened by the other person's necessary growth. What is experienced by one as an inner push to change is perceived and reacted to by the other as a threatening violation of a former trusted agreement. Furthermore, the threatened partner will attempt to hold the other in place as if he or she is a possession. Often there is jealousy of people and/ or events in the other's life that are associated with the threatening change. Each of these "outsiders" is a potential invader of the citadel of security we have fortified with the marriage vows and the threatened partner will see and often attempt to convince the other that they are unworthy if not dangerous.[9]

When one person in the marriage is threatened, the ensuing behavior can be anything from quiet withdrawal to rage. Although the Goulds were not speaking of situations where violence results, it is easier to understand the scenario in such extreme instances. I am referring here to domestic violence and what often happens when a woman steps out of her "assigned" role as primary nurturer and support to her husband and children and takes a different direction with her life.[10] She may go to work or develop new friends outside the marriage or any number of initiatives that indicate to the husband that he is not as important to her as he was. When a husband with unresolved childhood issues reacts violently to a wife's attempts to grow, then the problem compounds and grows into an unmanageable situation. Ultimately, what the wife wants is to be free of the husband's tyranny, or what she perceives as tyranny.

9. Gould and Gould, *Personal Growth and Marital Consequences*, 4.

10. I refer to a woman here because more than 90 percent of reported cases are of women being abused by their partners or spouses. PASCH (www.peaceandsafety.com) and RAVE (www.theraveproject.com) have up-to-date statistics on domestic violence.

On the other side often the freedom we seek from our own con-
trolling internal images is transformed into seeing freedom from
our spouses and thereby the avenue to marital misery is opened.
The one attempting to loosen attachments to archaic or outmod-
ed behavior or thought patterns will project the resistance to that
change onto the spouse. The reason for this is that it is far more
difficult to understand the source of resistance to the felt need to
change as residing in ourselves than it is to identify it as outside.

To see it in ourselves obviously makes us the embodiment of a
contradiction. For we must see ourselves at one and the same time
as fervently desiring change and obstinately standing against it.
This developmental conundrum is the one we must solve if relationships are to survive the normal process of individual growth
and transformation.[11]

To solve this "developmental conundrum" requires two mature individuals communicating on an equal level. This maturity is often not present in marriages, especially at a time when individual growth is imminent.
In my own marriage, when I began to change, neither I nor Gary knew
what was happening. I was restless and unhappy, but totally ignorant of
what the source of my problem was. Gary was afraid of what was happening to our marriage, so he clammed up, but hinted at the fact that I was the
problem. Had we known what the Goulds were explaining in their article,
my confusion and Gary's fears could have been alleviated.

An additional problem in our mix was the church to which we belonged. Instead of helping us through the conflict, the unwritten, but
clear, teachings stated that Christians solve their problems simply by
praying and reading the Bible. At the time, it was not acceptable to go for
counseling; that would be a sign of weakness, or even worse, an admis-
sion that one was not praying or reading the Bible as much as necessary.
The only way a couple with such a convoluted scenario being played
out in their lives could survive is through faith, a strong commitment
to remaining in the marriage, and a practice of forgiving one another
(Eph 4:32).[12] Our determination to remain in the marriage through this
precarious stage in my life was the key to our continual development
as individuals and to the creation of a strong marriage that could last
through the decades.

11. Gould and Gould, *Personal Growth and Marital Consequences*, 5.

12. "Be kind to one another, tenderhearted, forgiving one another, as God in Christ
has forgiven you."

During my long midlife transition, I wrote few memos regarding my marriage, but, in 1985, at age forty-one, when I felt my crisis was finally over, I began to record some of my thoughts on the topic. The memo included here gives a more positive assessment of my marriage. Our hard work was finally paying off. I was reflecting on my marriage because it was our anniversary.

> August 30, 1985
> Re: On marriage
> Today I've been married 22 years—more than half of my life. And it's time for some reflections on married life.
> There's no doubt in my mind that the past six months have been some, if not completely, the best of my married life. These past months have certainly not been free of problems—far from it. We've had more financial problems and reasons to worry than ever before because Gary's been out of a job for over a year. We've spent most of our savings (house equity) and we're living in the most crowded housing situation ever, but still, these months have been happy. . . .
> What brought about the change? Several factors contributed: moving across country, being nearly incapacitated by poor health, losing my grandfather, getting away from job and church pressures. But, the biggest factor of all was the realization that my husband needed me. He needed my support, attention, and love at the same time I needed these things. We clung together to survive a series of crises in our lives. . . . We needed each other, we needed other people, and, most of all, we needed God.
> Gary's faith, which had always been stronger than mine, wavered during this time. And I had to be strong and was the one who finally brought him around. We've become more and more alike in our beliefs. It's a reciprocal arrangement, too. He's helped me where I'm weak, and I've helped him where he was weak.
> That's why marriage is so valuable for the complete development of the self. Opposite traits in partners complement each other, bringing about two more complete selves. This is true, though, only when two partners are willing to sacrifice and allow some experimentation—time to find oneself.
> I wonder how many married people allow each other the time to explore, ultimately giving them the freedom to grow? I doubt very many. The outcome is so rewarding, worth all we've been through. We're now content; goal-oriented; more giving to our children, each other, and friends; and looking forward to the years ahead.

This memo still followed my pattern of a "happy ending," but it was closer to reality than most of my previous endings. I had identified some key elements in keeping a marriage together. The first factor in creating and maintaining a strong marriage relationship is that both partners are committed to making the marriage work from the beginning of the relationship. Commitment must remain an unchangeable fact. When both parties in a marriage are committed to making it work, the issue becomes how to make it work. This requires attention to strategies, something that most of us can learn with a lot of hard work. But, each couple has to come up with their own set of solutions, focus on being mature in how they relate to each other, and communicate to each other what they need from the relationship. Otherwise, neither person in the relationship will ever reach full development potential.

11

Authentic Christian Women

> I've discovered that the more I am forced to be in a place where I
> have to wear a mask, the more I crave the quiet time away from ev-
> eryone, just being myself. And, the older I get, the more important
> it is for me to have this quiet time. In fact, I think I have reached a
> point in my life where I will no longer be able to wear the mask for
> more than a few minutes at a time.[1]

I HAVE GRADUALLY DEVELOPED a great deal of respect for women in
general. From interviews I have done, life narratives written by my
students, relationships at work, and long-term friendships, I now realize that life is difficult for virtually all people. But, I can relate more to
women's suffering because of similar personal experiences. I have also
learned from my research, life experiences, and study of the Scriptures
that the more life challenges us, the stronger we become.[2] The pathway
from bewilderment to clarity is never easy, but most of us make it and
come out of it ready to help others navigate their lives. I adamantly believe we can be much more effective helpers once we discover who we
are, remove the masks worn because of social expectations, and thus
become *authentic*.

Authenticity is a term often found in women's psychological literature. Betty Clare Moffat, an author of several inspirational books,
describes an authentic woman beautifully:

> When I think of mature authenticity, I think of a painting I once
> had on the wall of a home that burned down years ago. The paint-

---

1. Memo to myself, March 14, 2003.

2. See Rom 5:3: "And not only that, but we also boast in our sufferings, knowing that
suffering produces endurance." See also Jas 1:2–3: "My brothers and sisters, whenever
you face trials of any kind, consider it nothing but joy, because you know that the test-
ing of your faith produces endurance."

ing was of golden, endless wheat fields, fat, thick strokes of shades
of sun and late high summer that matched the sun that shone on
the figure of a woman, indistinct in age, who stood in the middle
of the golden grain, raising her arms to the clear blue sky.

I am that woman. Perhaps you are too. After years of exposure to the merciless elements, to the sway and the turning of the
seasons, we have come to the end of summer. We have come to
the time of harvest. We have come into our full maturity. Like a
cornucopia of harvest grains and vegetables, we are full, bursting,
overflowing with plenty onto the tables of Thanksgiving.[3]

My definition of female authenticity is a woman who is mature and
feels comfortable being herself regardless of her circumstances. This
trait can be seen easily in a woman's face once you become acquainted
with it. I remember an elderly woman whom I knew in the 1970s and
early 1980s who just radiated confidence and general disregard for what
others thought of her. At the time, I did not have a word for her state of
contentment, but I now believe the source of her confidence was that
she knew exactly who she was. She was an authentic woman! I recall
a statement she made when I asked her to help with some project at
church: "I don't want to get involved; I'm ready for a rest." At the time,
I was frustrated, but now understand why, at age eighty-four, she felt it
was time for someone else to do what she had already spent a lifetime
doing. Unlike so many younger women, she had no trouble distinguish-
ing between what she must do for herself and what others expected of
her, and then she had no trouble saying no.

As I studied psychological theories of how women develop from
childhood to old age, I acquired a clearer picture of the unfolding process that brings about more knowledge of oneself and the surrounding
environment. Consequently, women develop a more mature identity,
which they describe as a feeling of wholeness. A woman gradually becomes comfortable in her own skin. As she progresses through life, she
becomes continually more aware of her "real self," who she is without the
facade created when she attempts to fulfill societal expectations. As time
passes and life experiences help her become aware of her limitations and
strengths, a woman is able to distinguish between who she really is—her
authentic self—and the roles she has been fulfilling in response to others' expectations. Her identity, then, becomes a reflection of what she

---

3. Moffat, *An Authentic Woman*, 21.

wants for herself, what is vital in her life, and what she cherishes, instead of what others have chosen for her.

In most instances, the things that have always been in her life—continuity—are buried in the unconscious portion of her psyche or forgotten because of numerous demands from "others." In an attempt to bring to the surface that which has been buried, many women must undergo an active "search for self" or a quest for meaning or self-understanding, though they are seldom sure of what they are seeking when they are in the midst of the process.

Among the women I studied, those who were in the midst of or had previously had a traumatic transition were those with values and roots that dictated a lifestyle dramatically different from the one they found themselves living out. My favorite example of this is Wilma,[4] mentioned previously in this book, who took a position as a high-profile broadcaster adapting an image dictated by others. Because she was not happy in her job, she struggled for years to find her authentic self. Once she found her ideal position among the working poor, she worked long hours because she was living out what she valued most. Wilma, like myself and other women I encountered, had inadequate role models to live in the society created by social movements in the 1960s and 1970s. For these, the search for self was painful, and achieving a mature or integrated identity was slow. But, once they worked through the process, they came out feeling quite content with their lives and ready to help others with their struggles.

As I gained insight into the process that women go through to become authentic, I began to realize that what I had needed, as a young woman, were role models of Christian women from whom I could learn. Because of my combined roles of wife, mother, student, and breadwinner, I could not relate to women in the traditional stay-at-home position. I needed to know how Christian women living in a non-traditional lifestyle managed their role in the church. Basically, I was trying to answer one underlying question: Do Christian women go through the same developmental process as the women I had interviewed, and, if so, how do they resolve their issues of identity and worth? Are their lives fulfilled, or are they simply keeping silent as I had?

4. Wilma (a pseudonym) struggled for nearly twenty years to find her authentic self, acquired only after she began to work with the type of people with whom she grew up in New York City: the working poor, people who had jobs but did not make enough money to survive.

WHAT IS A CHRISTIAN WOMAN'S PLACE
IN THE TWENTY-FIRST CENTURY?

When I turned sixty, I realized that, if I was ever going to determine any absolutes about women's lives, it had better be soon. For twenty-eight years, I had been questioning my life and researching the identity development process of women. I collected the life stories of more than sixty women, read numerous biographies of women, and studied the lives of women found in the Bible. In addition, I spent hours reading and discussing with my husband and friends the controversial Scriptures regarding women's role in the home and church. After all this, I cannot say I had discovered "The Truth" about the topic, but many pieces of the puzzle began to fall into place.

One of my most reliable findings is that every woman is different: She has a unique genetic makeup, a unique childhood socialization resulting in a particular set of skills and values, and varied, unique adult experiences that guide her life choices. If every woman is unique, then no one other than the woman herself and her closest acquaintances have a right to suggest how she should live her life. Each woman is responsible for managing a life that works for her and her family. No other man or woman can make these life decisions for her—but a Christian woman must continually ask herself how she can use her unique skills to serve God.

How can a person accomplish this if she is not clear what her uniqueness is? Uniqueness is discouraged by so many Christians. Our traditions are often treated as if they are as immutable as Scripture, and those who do not fit the mold are ostracized or ignored. As I interviewed women over the years and encountered Black Christian women who had a different story to tell, I realized how absurd it is that women have been told over the years to all be alike—to focus primarily on being a perfect wife and mother. Unlike many white, middle-class Christian women I have known who were told they must focus their primary energies on their children and husbands, cooking and cleaning, making things pleasant for others, and organizing social activities, to name a few, the Black Christian women I encountered were socialized to believe they can follow whatever path they want, and God will show them the way. Are we talking about two different Gods here? If not, one has to wonder how one group of people, following the same Bible, could have so narrowly interpreted women's roles in the home, the church, and society.

If women could be like men and choose how to serve based on their talents, as the Bible instructs,[5] what would we be doing? All kinds of things, because our talents often emerge from our experiences as children. The integration of our values, interests, skills, and talents, along with teachings from our subculture, help us form a core identity. That core determines how we should serve God. An identity core begins in early childhood and often revolves around some aspect of family life. A perfect example of this is Lena, a forty-two-year-old woman whose identity stemmed from her roots in an African American community in the South:

> Well, you see, being Black is so much a part of me, and growing up in the South at that time, it is and always was such a source of pride. The other thing was that we had a large, very strong, cohesive Black community, especially in the town that I grew up in. Now, I don't feel the same type of camaraderie with Blacks in the North and I think it's because they haven't had to struggle the way we struggled in the 50s. . . . I'm not surrounded by Black people the way I was when I grew up, and, over the course of years, you begin . . . when you are separated from people who are exactly like you, I guess, or I don't know what it is, but you begin to miss it and you long for it again.

As mentioned earlier, my core identity came from roots in a farming community. I had a childhood of watching ordinary people help each other survive because they cared about each other, not because they had church programs and edicts telling them what they were supposed to do. They attended church, but lived out their beliefs and values among their own neighboring farm families. My dad would give his last dollar to anyone who needed it, and my mother was a wonderful cook and continually shared her good food with others. My identity, because of early exposure to starving children in India in contrast to my family's wealth of home-grown, home-cooked food, resulted in a desire to help those less fortunate than me—first, children in India, and then, as I revised my dream, women and children in my own community who were struggling. My unique core identity dictated how I should serve God. I believe this is true for everyone. To be content, each person must live out his or her own identity, not what others plan for them.

---

5. See 1 Cor 7:7: "Each has a particular gift from God, one having one kind and another a different kind."

In the Scriptures, we are told that older women should teach the younger women—but does that mean older women should present only one formula that works for all? So often, I feel that women who teach and advise others use only their own narrow experiences as a model, rather than acknowledging a person's unique talents as the basis for determining the nature of their service to God. Using our individual God-given talents is also scriptural, as we are frequently reminded by the parable of the talents in Matthew 25. Also, 1 Corinthians 12 presents an in-depth study of spiritual gifts and how they differ among individuals:

> Now concerning spiritual gifts . . . there are varieties of gifts, but the same Spirit, and there are varieties of services, but the same Lord, and there are varieties of activities, but it is the same God who activates all of them in everyone. To each is given the manifestation of the spirit for the common good. To one is given through the Spirit the utterance of wisdom, and to another the utterance of knowledge according to the same Spirit, to another faith by the same Spirit, to another gifts of healing by the one Spirit, to another the working of miracles, to another prophecy, to another various kinds of tongues, to another the interpretation of tongues. All these are activated by one and the same Spirit, who allots to each one individually just as the Spirit chooses. (1 Cor 12:1–11 NRS)

How can Christian leaders read the Bible verses on spiritual gifts, and yet keep women in their very narrow role of service in traditional ways? For example, in the congregation my husband and I have attended for more than twenty-five years, the majority of women have been involved with traditional female duties, such as teaching children, cooking, and serving meals for congregational events. Within this church, there are many professional women who are leaders in their workplaces and communities, but, until very recently when our elders implemented a major change in policy, they sat silent during the worship service except for singing and an occasional prayer. At the same time, any man regardless of his training or knowledge can participate in a public role. The contradiction was frustrating at the least and, at times, left women discouraged and even angry. Contradictions like this, and the inattention of church leaders to these contradictions, I believe have chased many highly skilled and deep-thinking women away from our churches and possibly away from their marriages.

UNIQUE WAYS TO LIVE AND SERVE

Several wise women have helped me understand my role in life as a Christian woman and see how a woman with nontraditional, rather unique talents can survive within a conservative Christian church. One thing that has benefited me the most was to know that other women have struggled as I have, that they did not automatically know as young, inexperienced people how to live their lives. They had difficulty making their marriages work and some had trouble finding their place in the church, and yet, they remained faithful. I have learned from their cumulative struggles. From my mother, I learned how to work hard, really hard, regardless of how you feel at the time. I also learned from her how to survive the loss of a loved one. My dad was killed in a car accident when she was only forty-eight years old, and she remained strong until she died at age eighty-seven. From my grandmother and some of my aunts, whose marriages were less than ideal, I learned what commitment in marriage really means—it means that you do everything in your power to stay with a man, even when he is not necessarily worthy of you, and you keep working to make things better.

One woman who has taught me a lot about Christian living is Emma.[6] She was blessed enough to be born into a family with economic stability and seldom lacked the material things in life that many never acquire. But her financial security did not shield her from suffering. It took her until past midlife to discover who she really was and what her talents were. In her seventies, she said that she "grew up in a box with the top on—I was a loner and a late bloomer. But praise be to God, I am blooming." She had to learn, after two disappointing marriages, that she must not turn inward and feel sorry for herself, but "turn outward to others." To survive a difficult transition, she said she counted her blessings:

> I read Psalms. I put stick-ums on my bathroom mirror such as, "Thy will, not mine, be done," "This, too, will pass," "One day at a time," and "Bloom where you are planted."
>
> I rededicated my life to the Lord and entered a new chapter in my life. Rising from the ashes, as it were, has taken time, and is an ongoing journey. I am stronger spiritually, and I press on daily to become closer to him and do his will. I use the talents God has bestowed on me: photography, gardening, and the written words. These are all hobbies—and therapy as well.

6. A pseudonym.

Until her health problems became unmanageable, Emma used her artistic talents and her money to serve God. She quietly helped others with their life issues, giving both encouragement and financial support as it was needed.

Another Christian woman who lives in my neighborhood has often been a lifesaver for me. She is a wonderful listener and completely non-judgmental. She has served as a sounding board numerous times for me and probably for many other women in our fellowship. She continually serves others in her own way, and most do not even know she is serving because of her meekness and humility.

Another woman who has helped me focus on what is important in life is Arvelia.[7] At this writing, she is eighty-nine years old and still an encouragement to others. But, she is not only encouraging; she also follows the Biblical instruction to confront others about what they are doing wrong in their Christian journey. It takes a very special person to do this and have her rebukes accepted. I interviewed her just prior to her eightieth birthday and now use her words to teach others, including my undergraduate students, when the topic of religion, spirituality, and wisdom is broached. One of the most inspiring things about Arvelia is her love for God and her complete lack of fear of death and dying. She repeatedly tells me this. I think she does not fear death because she truly believes she has had such a good life.

> I have really begun to feel that I've had a full life and I feel that I'm in the sunset stage—naturally, I know this. I feel I've been blessed, and I've had some rough, rugged roads to travel through, but I ended up feeling very fulfilled with family. I have a church family that I love, and I feel loved.
>
> So, anyway, I feel really content, at peace. I mean, as much as I know how to be. I'm not worried, not troubled in any way. I've unfilled wishes, but they are long gone by; I don't have them any longer. I'm just happy to be here, and I'm looking forward to my going away. I'm not rushing it or anything; I don't know how to, but I know it will be taken care of when the time comes. And so, I just do the best I can.

These words of faith come from a woman who, as a Black child in the South, endured much.

---

7. Arvelia Mack has given me permission to use her real name. She lives in Hartford, Connecticut.

My brother passed. My baby sister passed. My twin sister passed. My older sister was alive . . . and then she had a lot of children. There wasn't very much she could do. She could see to my mother for six months at her house, and then she moved back to her own house, and I stayed there [with my mother].

They all passed away as babies, all but my twin sister. Back then, you would have had to be there to see, people had those cracks and things in their houses. People would take colds and it was just really bad. You didn't know sometimes because you couldn't get to the doctor most of the time. It was rough back there in those times. You hear them talk about Mississippi and Georgia. It was worse than anywhere. It was terrible in most of those places.

At age ten, Arvelia's parents separated. At age twelve, she began working in the cotton fields, ten hours per day, and received only fifty cents a day.

I went to school after the cotton would be through picking. You started the last of August and picked until it was out in February or March or whenever. They weren't sending children up. You lived so far from where the school would be, and you had to cross sloughs, ditches, and things, and the water would get up, and you didn't get to go that many days out of those few months that you would go to school. They wouldn't take you out of the field. Then, it wasn't [expected] that when school started, all the children went to school.

When you suffer so much throughout life, it often causes you to have faith in God, and, therefore, to look forward to the end when you will be with God and not have to suffer any more.

One thing I've learned a lot as I've grown older: My faith is much stronger, because I didn't always believe it as much as I believe it since I've lived this long and I've read it [the Bible] daily. I believe it more because I understand it better. Other books that have been written have helped me to be; it's almost like your meal. I'm thirsty and hungry for it. I have to have it every day, all through the day. I believe that he hears, and I can just look around me and see all the things that were created that man didn't have anything to do with it. And I can certainly believe it. . . .

I know he really hears prayers and answers prayers according to his will, and he doesn't leave anyone out. Everyone he loves, and I believe that, because he made everyone. I guess putting all these things together, it comes together, and it makes me feel more sure that this is real.

The unwavering faith in God that Arvelia and other mature Christian women practice has helped many younger women deal with their own suffering and uncertainty.

COMMON THREADS AMONG WOMEN

While every woman is unique and should live her life accordingly, nearly every woman I have encountered through my research or daily living has lived her life based on a set of themes—what I call *threads of continuity*— that began in childhood and continued throughout her lifespan. And these threads are not unique for every woman. There are similarities that make it possible for us to understand and learn from each other.

These threads are themes that begin as a piece of a woman's life and ultimately become a primary source of her identity. Nurturing and caring for others is a theme that many women share, whether they work outside the home in demanding jobs or are full-time homemakers. But nurturing must be considered more broadly than our society usually defines it. There are many ways to nurture other than taking care of husbands and small children in a home setting. It includes working for a broader, more encompassing cause than one's own family, and often involves empowering other women. This truth comes across unmistakably nearly every time I interview or engage in an informal conversation with a woman. Women find ways to nurture at home, at work, and in community organizations. And, in this way, they find meaning.

FINDING MEANING THROUGH NURTURING

Women who seem to be successful at making decisions about what is truly important in life engage in what I have labeled *value-driven nurturing*. This concept, which can be defined simply as living out your values by helping others, is tied to a person's specific life experiences. As can be seen from Wilma's story, mentioned in previous chapters, becoming very specialized or focused in your nurturing or empowering is often a result of conflicting or contradictory experiences that help women clarify values. Wilma's life experiences culminated in what we often refer to as a midlife crisis, but most people's stories are not has dramatic. In fact, I've been struck by how relatively small cumulative events can initiate big changes in people's lives or serve as catalysts for personal insight and growth.

Helen[8] is a good example of value-driven nurturing. She has always been a people helper, but has become more passionate about it as she has matured. She both nurtures and empowers people as she works with those who are suffering the loss of a loved one through death, and when she works on community projects with the homeless.

> I like things where you end up helping other people. Give me a project where I am going to help someone, I don't care how many hours a day it takes, that is something I really, really enjoy doing.

In her job as a bereavement counselor at a mortuary, Helen extends her helping role to the ultimate:

> When that phone rings, everything else drops. That is the most important thing you can do right there is help a family who has lost a loved one. . . . They need people to lean on at this time. . . . You sit back and watch these people who are hurting. It's so awful. . . .
>
> It's so wonderful to be able to watch people come out of this terrible, terrible hurt. The hurt is tremendous; you can't concentrate on anything.

Here, Helen's nurturing empowers people to heal. Helping others has been a theme throughout Helen's life, a trait she inherited from her parents that was reinforced in adulthood through her own experiences. She attributes her desire to help people to her experience of having eight miscarriages before her first son was born, and to her son's serious illness at age six, which required him to be hospitalized for one year.

> My parents used to tell us that looks and money were not important . . . used to tell us that personality is the biggest thing and helping other people. . . . You can always look around and find people who are so much worse off than you are.

Helen's life illustrates how a woman can be quite content in a subordinate, nurturing role, but this is the case with only some of the women I encountered. Others were passionate about their work for other reasons—reasons tied to their lifelong values.

---

8. A pseudonym. Helen was a participant in my dissertation study completed in the 1990s.

PASSION FOR WORK OUTSIDE THE HOME

During my interviews with professional and accomplished women throughout the past twenty years, I have frequently come away deeply impressed by the passion they have for their work. Their passion arouses in me once again a desire to do something more worthwhile with my life. I want to be passionate about *my* work. And, it always leads to a question I have struggled with for many decades: How can a Christian wife who is told in the Bible to be submissive still be passionate about her work outside the home? Our legacy as Christian women causes us to drop our own work instantaneously when someone needs us, especially if this person is our child or grandchild. To be passionate about one's work requires that you remain focused a large portion of every day, but our families and communities have needs that continually get us off course. How can women "run with perseverance the race set before us" (Heb. 12:1) when we must repeatedly stop and minister to others' needs?

In attempting to answer this question of passion, I must return to another story. The most passionate woman I encountered through my study of biographies is Lucretia Mott. Born in 1793 into a strong Quaker family, her life resembled that of the "good woman" in Proverbs 31. She and her husband Thomas demonstrated how two people can both fulfill their own dreams while being exemplary partners and parents. Both Thomas and Lucretia became public speakers; the Quakers, at least during the Motts' lives, allowed women to speak in public. Their main concern was that of peace, but the Motts went further and promoted the rights of slaves and women. In spite of having a large family for whom they cared without the benefit of modern conveniences, they still managed to leave a lasting mark on society by their work in the public realm.

> Everyone who knew the Motts said it was a good marriage. They complemented each other in important ways. Although they were active in the same causes, there was no rivalry. Lucretia was the innovator, the spiritually gifted leader, James the writer of letters and petitions, the chair of the meetings. He was an important figure in his own right; had he not been married to Lucretia Mott he might have become more famous. The fact that he was able to accept her preeminence in a day when society frowned on such an arrangement and few male egos could endure the consequent bruising is a testimony to the largeness of his spirit and the depth of their love. In their private life, in everything that mattered, they were equal partners. Lucretia looked up to and respected

James and was tender of his dignity. If their enemies sometimes called him Mr. Lucretia Mott, neither of them seemed to care.[9]

After the birth of their first two children, Lucretia began to help her husband by working outside the home. She became a schoolteacher in Philadelphia, but soon became a spokesperson for the abolitionists.

> Meanwhile a resolution had been forming in the back of her mind. Why shouldn't she help too? Anna at two and a half was a bright child and was beginning to learn to spell a little. Tommy, at nine months, had said his first words. She had loved being with them, but she had to confess that the life of a full-time housekeeper was a bit confining. James frequently came home exhausted at night just when she was ready for some human company. Why shouldn't she copy her mother and work to augment the family income? (p. 34)
>
> She spoke again and again, finding it easier each time. Her messages were in essence simple ones: the importance of obedience, the need for strength from beyond, the priority of religious experience over cult and creed. She found, however, that even in the grip of inspiration she could draw from her reading and present her ideas logically.[10]

After the death of her young son, Lucretia stood up and said a prayer in a Quaker meeting. It was so moving that she was asked to speak again. Soon, she was "formally recognized as a minister, a tribute rarely paid to a young woman still in her twenties."[11] Ultimately, Lucretia gave birth to six children, but she never stopped learning. She read while she nursed babies.

> She read the complete works of William Penn, a large folio copy that she propped up on a pillow next to her chair. She also read Mary Wollstonecraft's *Vindication of the Rights of Woman*, and found herself in complete agreement with this first champion of equal rights.[12]

Because of the devastating death of her son and previous experience with untimely death, Lucretia became disinterested in "earthly pleasures" and turned to "a deepening spiritual life and a continuing search for the

9. Bacon, *Valiant Friend*, 31.

10. Ibid., 34.

11. Ibid., 37.

12. Ibid., 38–39.

path of duty."[13] In addition to her many contributions to the antislavery and peace movements, Lucretia was influential in the birth of a women's rights movement in both England and the United States. She served as a role model for younger feminists who did much of the actual work of organizing meetings and delivering public speeches.

How did she do it all? First of all, her husband was completely supportive of the work she did outside the home. Additionally, Lucretia had a "remarkable talent for simplifying housework."[14] She gave up "fancy stitching," but while she talked or attended meetings, she sewed or knitted. She was frugal and gave what she saved to charity for destitute African Americans. In spite of her busy life outside her family, Lucretia managed her household exceedingly well.

> This unceasing activity won Lucretia the reputation as being a housewife without equal. In a day when it was feared that if a woman had any interests outside of her family, the family was bound to suffer, her dual role as housewife and reformer was constantly praised. "She is proof that it is possible for woman to widen her sphere without deserting it, or neglecting the duties which appropriately devolve upon her at home," one editor wrote rather unctuously.

Lucretia was proud of her ability to manage. Still, she confessed that things occasionally got ahead of her. Sometimes James would put on a clean shirt, only to find its buttons missing. He was, she reported to her sister, "remarkably bearing . . . the most striking evidence of dissatisfaction is in finding the buttonless shirt thrown on the bed and another put on its place. . . ."

> Housekeeping in general seems to have served Lucretia as a physical outlet. Whenever she was particularly worried or angry, she threw herself with redoubled energy into baking, scrubbing, ironing, preserving. In a day when nice middle-class ladies were allowed no exercise, Lucretia found in her housework and her dozens of errands about the streets of Philadelphia the release she craved. Housework did not drain her; it recharged her batteries for more battles of the mind.[15]

13. Ibid., 40.
14. Ibid., 45.
15. Ibid., 68–69.

Women who engage in both passionate work and family nurturing have the psychological advantage of having multiple satisfying roles. One feeds the other. In Lucretia's case, her strong circle of family and friends gave her the energy to face public battles: "Her life at home continued to be a source of nourishment and strength, preparing her for the escalating battles that lay in store for her public self."[16] If a woman feels fulfilled in her domestic role, then she is more likely to find the time and energy to fulfill a second demanding role outside the family.

In my own situation, I discovered that I was more content with my family life when I spent some time each week pursuing my own passion for learning. I have often wondered where I found the energy to go to school when I was working outside the home and caring for a family of five, but I believe the "night away" energized me for what I had to face at work and home on a daily basis. It turned delayed gratification into a positive feeling, because I felt that I was doing something for myself that would eventually lead to a more fulfilled life.

As people age and have less energy, they must learn to focus on what is most important and to reduce their involvement in other endeavors. Lucretia, in her later years, had to do the same. Her health was not good, but her passions remained. She finally settled on one battle to fight:

> Overriding all these other interests, however, was the cause into which she poured the fire of her remaining years, the cause of peace. Her long, painful struggle with her principles during the Civil War had awakened within her a strong desire to devote the rest of her life to trying to make sure that war and its barbarities never came again.

I have encountered a few Christian women who are modern-day Lucretias. To accomplish what they want with their lives, they have first proven themselves as good wives, mothers, and traditional church workers. They delay their own life plans, making sure others are cared for. They steal a little time when they can to work on their passions. In other words, they "do it all" like the super moms of the 1980s—family, community, and church service, along with their own life's work, which stems from the unique talents and interests they use to serve God.

16. Ibid., 71.

12

A Woman's Relationship with God

A WOMAN'S RELATIONSHIP WITH God must take precedence over everything else—but there is a difference between our religion and our relationship with God. We can be faithful churchgoers, but still be *spiritually starved*. A memo I wrote to myself when I was in my fifties tries to explain it:

> Throughout the years that I was in a midlife transition, it never entered my conscious mind that the internal chaos I was experiencing had anything to do with spiritual deprivation. I knew it had to do with the religious beliefs that I felt the church had imposed on me, but the concept of *spiritual* development was something we seldom discussed. There were frequent references to a life after death, both heaven and hell; there were songs and Bible verses about loving and having faith in God; and there were long discussions about becoming a mature Christian. But, none of these was helping me to become a *spiritually deeper* being.
>
> We went to church, studied the Bible, and served others when a need was identified. And we prayed—at church, at meals, in devotionals. But, it seemed to me that we were playing roles—dramatizing a Christian role. We were "religious," but being religious does not necessarily mean someone is "spiritual."
>
> The music in the church we were attending at the time was not inspirational or uplifting to me, though it may have been to other people. I loved a full instrumental accompaniment to the music, something we did not have. I also loved to hear the close harmony that comes only from a well-trained singing group, not congregational singing. The fact that I could not find this spiritual fulfillment at church, as I supposed everyone else did, was making me feel guilty and was, therefore, contributing to my restlessness and feeling that there was something very wrong with me. . . .

What I discovered later was that attending church could not always be a spiritually uplifting experience for me. Everyone has a unique way of communicating with God that is developed from childhood on, and my technique was through music. When I listened to the religious music that I had listened to as a child, then a feeling of closeness to God was a natural outcome.

It was through the stories of African American women that I first developed a true understanding of what it means to have a strong relationship with God. When I began my research on women's identity, I had no idea that the topic of religion and spirituality would surface. But it did, in my very first interview and, over the years, in the majority of the interviews I conducted. One of the first things I discovered was that religion and spirituality are not the same concept for most people, and that everyone has his or her own way of defining these terms—which ranged from simply "going to church" to an in-depth conversation with God, who is "sitting right next to me on this sofa." Some of the expressions were negative, some neutral, and some extremely positive and inspiring.[1]

Nearly all African American women I have encountered through interviews and life in general speak freely of God and of spirituality. Many consider God as a powerful being who guides their every decision, and some believe that God has a life plan for them. Barbara, the youngest of the African American women I interviewed (age thirty-one), reported that her spirituality was instilled in her by her grandmother, and now it is something that she and her husband "just know is important."

> I think it's because I know how important God is in my life. My husband agrees, so our life is what all we can do to spread the message of God's love. . . . I am who I am and I am where I am because of my beliefs in God. Things that people attribute to luck or fate, I attribute to a plan mapped out for me by God.

Bell, a corrections officer, grew up with a father who preached Christian values and a mother "who prayed about everything." In adulthood, prayer became a natural source of strength when she was facing obstacles at work or at home. Likewise, Wilma, the executive director of a nonprofit organization, felt that God was instrumental in leading her to a job that was the right fit for her.

---

1. Burke, "Spirituality."

Belinda, whose life had been sprinkled with numerous crises and uncertainties, prayed to God for guidance for all decisions she made. A single mother with tremendous responsibility at home and in her job as a teacher in an inner-city community, she thinks that "prayer is constant, and I think that God is within you, and that as long as you carry consideration and love for other people, that he is working within your life." Because she felt that God takes care of her, Belinda tried to give to others what she received:

> There is a God; he takes care of me. . . . Even [with] the things that happen to me, I've always come out okay . . . and I want to give back just a little of what he's given me in my life, and every once in a while to just hug a kid and listen to them.

The overwhelming influence of God in the lives of the African American women in this study led me to ask Haley, a dean at a medical school, why African American women appear to be more spiritual than white women. Her answer was:

> I don't necessarily think we are more spiritual, but I think spirituality is closer to reality. To me, it's like God sitting over on the other end of the couch. I could sit here in this chair and rock and talk to God like God is sitting in this room with me. God's not a way off yonder somewhere. God is very close. God is very, very close. All I have to do is just be ready to talk to God. . . . You know what that goes back to? You know when you're little and you are cleaning up and your mother says, "Now, you have to dust under the bed, because even if I don't see it, God sees it." So I thought God was up under the bed with the dust bunny. It was just that real to me. I'd go to see if I could catch God under the bed. When I say God is there, it's not a God up in heaven or God away off down the street. God is everywhere.

More than one life story expressed a conflict between closeness to God or feeling the movement of the Spirit and the demands of marriage. One woman in her thirties compared her own church to that of her husband's, where she felt forced to attend. I summarized our conversation in a memo:

> At her church, "I felt like the Spirit was alive there." In her husband's church, "it was stifled, it was squelched. Put under a rock and told to be still." At first, she "held on to the things that I thought were right. . . . I would really have a lot of good feelings

about having been there at the Bible study, and it inspired me in a
lot of ways. Things I heard, I just said, 'Yes!' They registered with
my insides in a real meaningful way. . . .

I was not a part of his 'family.' . . . I felt real bitter about it. . . . I
really sometimes felt desperate. I didn't know what I could do. . . .
I just had nobody I could talk to. My prayers got deeper in my life
and were stronger than they had ever been in my life. . . . I came
to a point where I felt like there was a roadblock, that I could not
go forward, I just could not move unless I did something. . . . They
were just killing something in me. . . . It was a real killing-of-the-
Spirit kind of rightness.

The disagreement on where to attend church was tearing apart their
marriage, so someone had to yield:

Eventually, she gave in to her husband's way of thinking about
religion. "I set my jaw and did it. . . . I think I lost a lot of the fire
of my faith, I guess, because I started going on someone else's
coattails. . . .

It's hard for us to talk about it even now. Sometimes I feel like
it is all going to come back, like it is just waiting to spring on me,
if I start having doubts about what I believe . . . so I think he and I
have both pretty well avoided it. . . . I felt really cheated. . . . I was
cut off from these other friends, and I haven't talked to them since,
except maybe one time. . . . I think what happened, it hurt so much
that I just kind of closed it down. My prayers have not been as rich
. . . and I'm just kind of maintaining and barely that. . . . Lately it's
been, 'I need God, and why can't I get close again?' I'm just having
a struggle to get close again. . . . I go through the motions now, and
I hate that I have lost that" [feeling the Spirit was alive and a sense
of community with the people].

The purpose for giving in to her husband was to strengthen their
marriage, but it came at the expense of this woman's spiritual growth. It
took many years for her to feel comfortable in "his" church.

At the other end of the spectrum, Laura, an artist who had received
a good Catholic education, had left behind her family's religious values
and was in the process of constructing a new set for her family:

If you asked me to define God, I don't think I could . . . and yet
every time I'm in a real jam, like when my son was in the hospital, I
prayed. I don't know to whom; I just believe that there was nothing
else to be done but to pray, and you know, if it worked, it worked,
and it seemed to have worked. So again, I wouldn't deny it.

Laura's story, however, did not stop there. She was immersed in the process of trying to understand a contradiction she had encountered in her religious education and was using art to work through the issues. In her religious upbringing, she was taught to fear a judgmental God. She wanted to believe that he was a benevolent God and had spent much of her adult life trying to understand the contradiction between these early teachings and what her life experiences were telling her was the truth.

> [Y]ou can't grow up Roman Catholic and not feel guilty. The first thing they tell you, the very first thing you learn in religion is: Who made you? God made you. Why didn't he make you so you would be happy with him in heaven? And your body is evil, especially if you are a woman. . . . Eve was the one who caused the downfall of the whole human race. And growing up with nuns especially, they are very, very [blunt] about that.
>
> I can still remember the story the nun told us about how Jesus would come down and strike you dead if you did something horrible. And I could not [reconcile] the vengeful, horrible God that these nuns were talking about with the concept of a God that I was evolving out of, taking in the other half: the good, the provider, the creator of the world. There were too many conflicts.

This contradiction resurfaced after her son nearly died of injuries from a car accident. As she sat in his hospital room, she had time to meditate, and the questions that she needed to answer before moving on with her life began to crystallize:

> I could remember wanting very much to do some art, and I was at the point where I couldn't pull myself out of the . . . pain, the trauma, whatever. Watching your child suffer, struggle, is very, very painful and . . . instead I centered on thinking . . . in terms of properties, emotions, or what have you, of women and the experience of a woman, as a nurturer, as a teacher, as a mender . . . like what is the condition of a woman?

The question that emerged for Laura was whether women were evil, as Eve had been depicted in those childhood teachings, or good, as she felt she was as a mother. Mothers are "nurturers, teachers, menders, and they suffer much." Making sense of life through art, then, became a key for Laura. It gave her continuity, a sense of purpose, and a means for resolving religious issues from childhood. It helped her bring all of life's pieces together. Her personal philosophy began to take shape as is evidenced through what she said she was teaching her children:

> We are not religious; we don't practice any particular religion, but I saw to it, since we do live in a Christian country, my own kids were introduced to the Bible and things like that, but I always figured that religion is something that you acquire in the process of a lifetime. And you evolve what you need from it. . . . I keep telling my kids, it's more important to live your lives in such a way that you hurt no one than it is to go to church and pray and turn around and beat the heck out of the kid next door, or what not, or cheat on a test, or whatever. To be a good person is more important.

Laura's search for truth was still in progress when I completed the last interview with her. At age thirty-nine, she was continuing to work through her spirituality.

Regardless of the function of religion in the women's lives, religion or spirituality is connected in some way to their personal identity and search for meaning. Therefore, it is extremely important for women as they mature to clarify for themselves their core identity. An outcome of this process is often a deeper spiritual life.

13

Peeling Away the Masks

I T TOOK ME MORE than forty years to become the authentic person I
believe God intended me to be. In spite of a childhood where I was
drilled in the Scriptures and an adulthood focused on going to church
and serving others, I struggled with what my *specific* calling was. In
Ephesians 4, we are told to "Live a life worthy of the calling to which you
have been called" and to use our gifts to serve God. In the same chapter
in Ephesians, we are told that we should be maturing in Christ: "we must
no longer be children, tossed to and fro and blown about by every wind
of doctrine, by people's trickery, by their craftiness in deceitful schem-
ing. But speaking the truth in love, we must grow up in every way into
him who is the head, into Christ. . . ."

Because of my long personal struggle to find my true self, by middle
adulthood, I knew clearly who I was as a person, and I knew I had a
number of talents that I should be using to serve God. However, I could
not always fit my talents into the programs offered in the church with
which I worshipped. What I really have the talent for and love to do
is teach, but, since women have not been allowed to teach men, there
are few opportunities for me. I am limited to classes for women only,
which are seldom offered in a small congregation. Over the years, I have
had many ideas for educating people (not just women) on a variety of
topics, including marriage and family, human development, and parenting. Since I am well trained in that field and teach those subjects at the
university level, I feel I should be used in that capacity in the church.
For example, as Gary and I encounter couples wanting help with their
marriages, I think how good it would be to do some preventive work
by teaching couples how to resolve issues in their marriage before the
problems escalate to a place beyond help.

During the last few decades of my life, I have been able to use my talents in many small ways. I have always been interested in the inner city, and, although our church is not located there, through an acquaintance who worked at a homeless shelter, I used my writing skills to prepare grants. Because of contact with women who were abused both in and outside the church, I received domestic violence training and facilitated support groups in a women's shelter and in our local congregation. This interest helped me connect with other women in our congregation who were doing similar work in the community. We now have a core of women we can call upon if a need arises. I also use my own life struggles and education to help women progress through difficult midlife transitions.

For me, and, I believe, for many other people, it takes a good part of life to determine what our *unique* purpose on earth is. From a biblical standpoint, our purpose is tied to our specific talents and gifts (Eph 4:11–16): some are teachers; some are prophets, pastors, and evangelists. Beginning in early childhood, we learn about our world, ourselves, and others, but, for many of us, it takes decades to discover our talents and to determine how to use them to glorify God and reach our full potential. My desire to serve people came not just from my Christian heritage, but also from my family history and childhood socialization. There were many pieces to my identity that had to fit together before I could feel comfortable with myself and could clearly delineate who I was as a unique individual. Once I could define myself as an authentic person, I could serve God in a manner that I thought would please him.

Scripture also mandates that we be genuine or authentic. In 2 Corinthians 6:6, the word often translated as "genuine" literally means not wearing a mask or not being hypocritical:

> As we work together with him, we urge you also not to accept the grace of God in vain. . . . See, now is the acceptable time; see, now is the day of salvation! We are putting no obstacle in anyone's way, so that no fault may be found with our ministry, but as servants of God we have commended ourselves in every way: through great endurance, in afflictions, hardships, calamities, beatings, imprisonments, riots, labors, sleepless nights, hunger; by purity knowledge, patience, kindness, holiness of spirit, *genuine love*, truthful speech and the power of God. (2 Cor 6:1–7 RSV, italics added)

Therefore, I believe that understanding our purpose on earth requires being an authentic person. One of the greatest commandments is to love others, even our enemies—but that requires first loving ourselves, and we cannot love ourselves if we are not honest with ourselves. Romans 12:9 puts it simply: "Let love be genuine." To love genuinely, we must be authentic. To be authentic, we must peel away the masks acquired during childhood, adolescence, and early adulthood as we struggle to be the "good little girl" and "good woman" dictated by society, and, in many situations, by the conservative churches to which we belong.

Peeling away masks acquired from attempting to conform to others' expectations is a frightening experience and generally requires help from others. To do so, a woman must find a few people who can give her unconditional acceptance. In my case, I made my *own* friends—that is, I developed friendships that were not connected to my relationship with my husband. They were, for the most part, people who were not as "together" as most of our church friends appeared to be. They came from all walks of life, and most had been through a great deal of trauma. I vicariously learned from their experiences. They became what Roger Gould called "friends of growth."[1] They listened without judging and appeared not to be shocked by my need to explore life. These friends gave me the courage to take small steps toward independence. They gave me a safe place to explore and create my own identity. To return that favor has become one of my life goals. The sense of purpose I so desperately sought when I was in my early thirties at last was present.

Because of my lonely attempts to discover my place in the world, particularly in the church and my marriage, I realized how important it is for Christian women to help other women. We need to open ourselves up, talk about our own struggles—our weaknesses and fears—as well as how we arrive at solutions. If we just listen, we discover that nearly every woman has "secrets" she needs to share, problems she thinks are unanswerable, and deep pain beginning in childhood and continuing throughout her life that has changed the course of her future. We simply must listen to each other's stories!

1. Gould, "Transformations during Early and Middle Adult Years," 223.

14

Dream Revisited

Since this book began with the first memo I wrote in 1976, I think it is appropriate for it to end with the last few memos I wrote on this topic, which help to show how far I have come in understanding my role as a Christian woman in today's world. It took thirty years of introspection, exploration, soul searching, and writing to find my secure and productive place in the world. It is interesting to observe after all these years how my life story appears to have been carefully planned—and perhaps it was. God works in mysterious ways! In memos written in the past few years, I managed to put to rest most of the agitation and uncertainty regarding my calling. Because I was nearing age sixty, I was beginning to think about how many years I had left to complete my goals. It was time to integrate all my life experiences into one meaningful whole. In 2003, at age fifty-nine, I wrote a memo summarizing my search for self and authenticity. Then, at age sixty, a memo showed that there is hope for all of us to find contentment eventually, regardless of how many times we have to change paths along the way.

April 29, 2004
Re: Being content

In the past week, two incidents have given me a lot to think about. First, when I interviewed for a part-time teaching position, the woman interviewing me, close to the end of our session, said: "You look so happy." I was totally surprised, because I have never had anyone say that to me before. We had been talking about my desire just to teach and not work any longer as a training consultant.

Then, this week, after a class I taught at another college, one student stayed behind to talk to me about her assignment. The first thing she said was, "Do you go to church?" I told her that I do, and she said, "I knew the first time I saw you that you went to

134

church." She said she could tell by the look on my face. Then she said, "I could hear it in your voice." She had called me to discuss the class before we met in person.

These two incidents felt very strange because I have never felt that "going to church" has much to do with being a spiritual person. Throughout the last forty years of my life, I've questioned frequently the value of church attendance and have spent a considerable amount of time writing about this subject, as well as reading academic articles on the difference between spirituality and being "religious." The student who asked about my church attendance was really speaking about something else. She was referring to my behavior and actions in a setting other than the church—in the world, so to speak.

My reaction to these two incidents is one of relief. Have I finally reached a point in my life where I can be myself and be appreciated for it? I have struggled since age thirty-two to discover who I am and why I am so restless and anxious about my "self" in relation to others. I feel like I'm at home—finally. I'm content with who I am and feel good about what I'm doing with my life at the moment, what I've accomplished in the past, and I look forward to what's ahead.

And, because I have diligently studied human development for most of my adult life, I also feel confident that I know exactly why I feel good at this point in my life. I can describe in depth the process I have gone through to find my comfort zone, and I have discovered the vocabulary to explain how a person goes from immaturity, and, thus, insecurity, to maturity or a place in life where one is able to feel authentic. This end product of being your real self is a feeling of contentment with the person you are—and, yes, even happy.

The last memo written on my own development process was a life summary. I finally could put all the pieces of the tapestry together and see exactly what I had been through.

December 4, 2006
Re: Renewing the spirit through writing
From 1976 to 2006, I spent thirty years in therapy, writing therapy, done in my own home, regulated by myself. It kept me sane, but only postponed the inevitable. There had to come a time when I became my own person. Living my life under someone else's prescription was deadly. The story I have been writing for thirty years has many themes, but one dominates: how the teach-

ings of a traditional society and conservative church squelched the spirit and dreams I had as a child. The "service to others" mentality sounds like exactly what I wanted to do with my life, but it was always someone else's dream I was helping to fulfill, not mine.

How did it all play out?

In adolescence, I needed a moratorium to decide what to do with my life, but instead got married, had three children, and worked to put my husband through graduate school to earn two degrees.

In 1976, I again needed a moratorium. I was drained from working, caring for young children, and helping my husband fulfill his dream. But I began writing, trying to clear the cobwebs from my mind and focus on what I wanted to do with my life (someday!).

From 1976 to 1984, I kept trying to find my way to fulfillment, but delayed gratification was the practice that kept me going. Someday, it was going to be "my turn." And I continued to write memos to myself, sharing them with no one.

The years from 1984 to 1994 were spent in graduate school to prepare myself for a new dream: helping women like myself navigate the muddy waters of life.

From 1995 to 2002, I tried to find a teaching job, but couldn't move from the area because my husband had a good job. So, I began teaching part time (delayed gratification again) and kept making money for the family to survive. I kept my dream alive by writing, this time working on a book.

From 2002 to 2006, I cut back on paid employment to help with grandchildren—no extra time for me. Teaching part time and loving it. Book is still in the making.

Good things come to those who wait! I can now write a new chapter to my life story. Through one of the women who inspired me to write this book, Catherine Clark Kroeger, I met Leela Manasseh, a woman from India who has facilitated the fulfillment of my earlier dream to help children in that country. I met her when I was around sixty years old. A few months before I turned sixty-five (May 2009), Leela stayed in our home for a few days, and the plans to go to India became a reality. In November 2009, Gary and I spent eight days in India and have since become involved in Leela's ministry with women and children there.

When I met women in India, I told some of them my story and how I had finally found my calling to work with women, both Christian and non-Christian, who were suffering. One woman asked what I planned to do with what I had learned from my life experiences. Did I plan to write a book? I told her I was in the process of doing so. They seemed satisfied that I was fulfilling my dream in a way that others could gain from it. My continual habit of delayed gratification had kept my dream alive until I could revisit it. As I write this final chapter, I do not know the outcome of revisiting my dream, but because of the long quest I have been through, I feel confident there will be a happy ending.

Bibliography

Adelson, J., ed. *Handbook of Adolescent Psychology*. New York: Wiley & Sons, 1980.

Andelin, Helen. *The Fascinating Girl*. Santa Barbara, CA: Pacific, 1970.

———. *A Fascinating Womanhood*. Santa Barbara, CA: Pacific, 1971.

———. "Scarecrow and Mrs. King." *Marriage, the Fascinating Way* Web site, February 2002. http://www.fascinatingwomanhood.net/2002/200202main.html.

Bacon, Margaret Hope. *Valiant Friend: The Life of Lucretia Mott*. New York: Walker, 1980.

Boggs, Sue Hill. *Is a Job Really Worth It?* Fort Worth, TX: Quality Publications, 1979.

Brown, Lyn Mikel, and Carol Gilligan. *Meeting at the Crossroads*. New York: Ballantine, 1993.

Burke, Patricia C. "Spirituality: A continually evolving component." In *Religion, Belief, and Spirituality in Late Life*, edited by L. Eugene Thomas and Susan A. Eisenhandler, 113-136. New York: Springer, 1999.

Buscaglia, Leo. *Living, Loving, and Learning*. New York: Henry Holt, 1982.

———. *Love*. New York: Holt, Rinehart & Winston, 1972.

Chafe, William H. *The American Woman: Her Changing Social, Economic, and Political Roles, 1920-1970*. New York: Oxford University Press, 1972.

Chodorow, Nancy. *The Reproduction of Mothering*. Berkeley: University of California Press, 1978.

Coontz, Stephanie. *The Way We Never Were: American Families and the Nostalgia Trip*. New York: BasicBooks, 1992.

Coontz, Stephanie. *The Way We Really Are: Coming to Terms with America's Changing Families*. New York: BasicBooks, 1997.

Diamond, Neil. "I Am, I Said." Uni Records, 1971.

Dowling, Colette. *The Cinderella Complex, Women's Hidden Fear of Independence*. New York: Summit, 1981.

Edmonds, Leon. "The Minister's Wife." *Christian Worker* 49, no. 9 (February 28, 1963), 3-6.

Epstein, C. F. *Woman's Place*. Berkeley: University of California Press: 1971.

Eriksen, J. A., W. L. Yancey, and E. P. Eriksen. "The Division of Family Roles." *Journal of Marriage and the Family* 41 (1979): 301-14.

Erikson, Erik. *Identity and the Life Cycle*. New York: International University Press, 1959.

———. *Identity: Youth and Crisis*. New York: Norton, 1968.

Feldberg, R. L., and E. N. Glenn. "Male and Female: Job versus Gender Models in the Sociology of Work." *Social Problems* 26 (1979): 524-35.

Fels, Anna. *Necessary Dreams: Ambition in Women's Changing Lives*. New York: Anchor, 2004.

Ferree, M. M. "Working-Class Jobs: Housework and Paid Work as Sources of Satisfaction. *Social Problems* 27 (1976): 431–41.

Freidan, Betty. *The Feminine Mystique*. New York: W. W. Norton, 1963.

Gatlin, Rochelle. *American Women since 1945*. Jackson, MS: University Press of Mississippi, 1987.

Gilligan, Carol. *In a Different Voice*. Cambridge, MA: Harvard University Press, 1982.

"Good Wife's Guide." *Housekeeping Monthly Magazine*, May 1955, n.p.

Gould, Renee V., and Roger L. Gould. *Personal Growth and Marital Consequences*. Unpublished article, 1976.

Gould, Roger. *Transformations*. New York: Simon and Schuster, 1978.

———. "Transformations during Early and Middle Adult Years." In *Themes of Work and Love in Adulthood*, edited by Neil J. Smelser and Erik H. Erikson, 213-237. Cambridge, MA: Harvard University Press, 1980.

Green, Marge. *What Are We Doing Here? A Book about Living as Christian Women*. Abilene, TX: Quality, 1972.

Gundry, Patricia. *Woman Be Free: The Clear Message of Scripture*. Grand Rapids: Zondervan, 1977.

Hall, C. S., and V. J. Nordby. *A Primer of Jungian Psychology*. New York: Penguin, 1973.

Hancock, Emily. *The Girl Within*. New York: Fawcette Columbine, 1989.

Hancock, Maxine. *Love, Honor, and Be Free*. Chicago: Moody, 1975.

Hess, B. B., and M. M. Ferree, eds. *Analyzing Gender: A Handbook of Social Science Research*. Newbury Park, CA: Sage, 1987.

Hymowitz, Carol, and Michaele Weissman. *A History of Women in America*. New York: Bantam, 1984.

Jack, Dana Crowley. *Behind the Mask: Destruction and Creativity in Women's Aggression*. Cambridge, MA: Harvard University Press, 1999.

———. *Silencing the Self: Women and Depression*. Cambridge, MA: Harvard University Press, 1991.

Jacobi, J. *The Psychology of Jung*. New Haven, CT: Yale University Press, 1943.

Janeway, E. *Cross Sections from a Decade of Change*. New York: William Morrow, 1982.

Jividen, Jimmy. "Glorious Woman." *Restoration Quarterly* 19, no. 3 (1976): 148–54.

Johnson, Allan G. "Patriarchy, the System: An It, Not a He, a Them, or an Us." In *Reconstructing Gender: A Multicultural Anthology*, 5th ed., edited by Estelle Disch, 98-106. Columbus, Ohio: McGraw-Hill Higher Education, 2009.

Josselson, Ruthellen. *Finding Herself: Pathways to Identity Development in Women*. San Francisco: Jossey-Bass, 1990.

Jung, Carl. *Memories, Dreams, Reflections*. New York: Vintage, 1965.

———. *Two Essays on Analytical Psychology*. 2nd ed. Princeton, NJ: Princeton University Press, 1953.

———. *The Undiscovered Self*. Boston: Little, Brown, 1957.

Kanter, R. M. *Work and Family in the United States: A Critical Review and Agenda for Research and Policy*. New York: Russell Sage Foundation, 1976.

LaHaye, Beverly. *The Spirit-Controlled Woman*. Eugene, OR: Harvest House, 1976.

Levinson, Daniel J. *Seasons of a Man's Life*. New York: Ballatine, 1978.

———. *Seasons of a Woman's Life*. New York: Ballatine, 1996.

———. "Women's Lives: Developmental and Social Perspectives." Presentation to the convention of the American Psychological Association, New York, August 1987.

Lightfoot, Neil R. *The Role of Women: New Testament Perspectives.* Memphis, TN: Student Association Press, 1978.

Lindbergh, Anne Morrow. *Gift from the Sea.* New York: Pantheon, 1955.

Lopata, H. Z., and B. Thorne. "On the Term 'Sex Roles.'" *Signs* 3 (1978): 718–21.

Mason, Karen Oppenheim, John Czajka, and Sara Arber. "Change in U.S. Women's Sex-Role Attitudes, 1964–1974." *American Sociological Review* 41, no. 4 (August 1976): 573–96.

Matthaei, J. A. *An Economic History of Women in America: Women's Work, the Sexual Division of Labor, and the Development of Capitalism.* New York: Schocken, 1982.

Miller, Jean Baker. *Toward a New Psychology of Women.* 2nd ed. Boston: Beacon Press, 1986.

Miller-McLemore, Bonnie F. *Also a Mother: Work and Family as Theological Dilemma.* Nashville: Abingdon, 1994.

Moffat, Betty Clare. *An Authentic Woman: Soulwork for the Wisdom Years.* New York: Simon and Schuster, 1999.

Moffatt, Mary Jane, and Charlotte Painter, eds. *Revelations: Diaries of Women.* New York: Random House, 1975.

Morgan, Marabel. *The Total Woman.* Old Tappan, N.J.: Revell, 1973.

Olds, Sally Wendkos. *The Mother who Works outside the Home.* New York: Child Study Press, 1975.

Oppenheimer, V. "The Sociology of Women's Economic Role in the Family." *American Sociological Review* 42 (1977): 387–40.

Peck, M. Scott. *The Road Less Traveled.* New York: Touchstone, 1988.

Pleck, J. H. "The Work-Family Role System." *Social Problems* 24 (1977): 417–27.

Ross, Cathy. "Separate Spheres or Shared Dominions?" *Transformation: An International Journal of Holistic Mission Studies* 23, no. 4 (October 2006): 228–35.

Rothman, Sheila M. *Woman's Proper Place: A History of Changing Ideals and Practices, 1870 to the Present.* New York: BasicBooks, 1978.

Rubin, Lillian B. *Women of a Certain Age: The Midlife Search for Self.* New York: Harper & Row, 1979.

Sterling, Dorothy. *Ahead of Her Time: Abby Kelley and the Politics of Antislavery.* New York: W. W. Norton, 1991.

Stookey, Noel Paul. "Wedding Song (There Is Love)." Public Domain Foundation, 1971.

Waite, Linda J. "Working Wives: 1940–1960." *American Sociological Review* 41, no. 1 (1976): 65–80.

Welter, Barbara. "The Cult of True Womanhood, 1820–1860." *American Quarterly* 18, no. 2 (1966): 151–74.